THE *AKITA* TODAY

Dave and Jenny Killilea

Ringpress

Published by INTERPET PUBLISHING
Vincent Lane, Dorking, Surrey, RH4 3YX
United Kingdom

Designed by Rob Benson

First Published 1998
Reprinted 2002
© 1998 RINGPRESS BOOKS
DAVE & JENNY KILLILEA

ISBN 1 86054 099 6

Printed and bound in Singapore
by Kyodo Printing Co

10 9 8 7 6 5 4 3 2 1

Ch. Am. Ch. Goshens Heir Apparent At Redwitch

23.9.1987 – 22.6.1997

Photographed at 9 ¹/₂ years.

This book is dedicated to the memory of 'Prince' for teaching us the true
meaning of the word Akita, and for leaving the breed
in Britain a legacy which benefited so many.

ACKNOWLEDGEMENTS

We send our sincere appreciation and thanks to the following:

To our daughters Emma and Jane and close friends, Joan Rushby, and Ian and Sue
Johnson for their encouragement and help in writing this book.
To Loren Egland of America and Margaret Hippolite of New Zealand for their
research and hard work.
To Catherine Bell and Bill and June Wynn for sharing their knowledge, experiences
and love of the breed with us over the years.
To Dr Malcoln Willis for the section on genetics.
To our great friend Dr Wayne Welch of Barbados for sharing our beliefs for the
past fifteen years.
To everyone else who has contributed information and photographs.
But mainly to our daughter Sam, who has suffered us, encouraged us, typed for us,
but most of all been there for us.

CONTENTS

INTRODUCTION   6
The great Sachmo; Influential imports; The advent of Rave.

Chapter One: ORIGINS OF THE AKITA   14
Hachi-Ko; The transition to America; The war years.

Chapter Two: THE AKITA AS A BREED   19
Colour; Character and temperament; Multiple ownership; The family pet;
Grooming; Exercise; Dominance; Training; Akitas with children; Akitas with
cats; The show or working dog.

Chapter Three: CHOOSING A PUPPY   29
Choosing a pet; Male or female; Finding a breeder; The show prospect;
Arriving home; House training; Feeding and exercise; Training and
socialization.

Chapter Four: CARING FOR YOUR AKITA   39
Nutrition and feeding; Dog foods; Supplements; Snacks and treats; Exercise;
Common ailments; Worming; Fleas and ticks; Blocked anal glands; Pressure
points; Sore testicles; Frozen tail; Popping hocks; Dog fights; Bloat;
Intussusception; Poisoning; Diarrhoea.

Chapter Five: THE AKITA STANDARD   49
The FCI Standard; The American Standard; The British Standard; Discussion
of the Standards.

Chapter Six: SHOWING THE AKITA   71
Preparation; Grooming; Bathing; Drying; Nails; Teeth; Ears; Coat Care; Ring
Training; Handling and Presentation; Moving your Akita.

Chapter Seven: JUDGING THE AKITA   87
Practicalities; Ring manners; Approaching the Akita; Merits *v* faults; Structure
and movement.

Chapter Eight: TIPS FROM THE TOP   95
Catherine Bell; Bill Wynn; Margaret Hippolite; David Killilea.

Chapter Nine: BREEDING AKITAS   108
Pedigrees and planning; Health and suitability; Breeding your bitch; The
mating; Conception to whelping; Giving birth; Rearing.

Chapter Ten: BREED ASSOCIATED CONDITIONS   120
Entropion; Ectropion; Progressive retinal atrophy; Microphthalmia; Hip
dysplasia; Panosteitis; Skin disorders; Mange; Auto-immune disorders; Vogt-
Koyanagi-Harada; Pemphigus Foliaceus; Auto-immune thyroid disease and
hypothyroidism.

Chapter Eleven: GENETICS AND THE AKITA   124
by Dr Malcolm B. Willis
Genetic make-up; Inheritance of coat; Inherited defects; Polygenic traits; Hip
dysplasia; Wither height; Heritability; Breeding to the Standard; Choosing
breeding stock.

Chapter Twelve: THE AKITA IN AMERICA   132
Early influences; Development of the breed; Transatlantic excitement; The
breed today; The show scene in America; The Points system; Classification;
Judging; Handling; The re-opening of the stud book.
Imports and Outcrosses in the USA *by Loren Egland*

Chapter Thirteen: THE AKITA IN BRITAIN   155
The influx of imports; The first breed clubs; Early show successes; Early
influential kennels; Important sires and dams; Breed development; The care
programme; Registrations; Help and education; Overflowing rescue; Full
circle.

Chapter Fourteen: THE AKITA AUSTRALASIA   173

INTRODUCTION

It is hard to believe that it is fifteen years since we were first introduced to this magnificent breed. The saying is true, time flies when you are having fun! It is very difficult starting in a breed when you can count the number of dogs already in the country on one hand and when all the depth of knowledge and experience lies thousands of miles away. However, our love and admiration for the Akita gave us a thirst for knowledge which became unquenchable.

We both have a history in dogs going back to the 1960s. David was brought up with livestock and, after handling pedigree bulls at shows, it was an easy progression to go on to handling dogs.

Bulldogs were his first love and, even to this day, nothing is guaranteed to melt his heart faster than a Bulldog puppy rolling on its back and waving its paws at him. After a period of some success, both breeding and showing, he then graduated to Rottweilers, a breed that the two of us love dearly and through which we first met.

David is an exceptionally good handler, seeming to have an immediate rapport with any dog he touches. Because of this, he soon gained a reputation for handling problem dogs, turning the fiercest into a pussy cat within minutes. I have often watched with bated breath as he has planted a huge kiss onto a snarling Rottweiler's

Co-author, David Killilea still handling the breed he started with. Shown here in 1996 with Ch. El Toro Jimmy Thunder en route to his title.

nose, only to see the dog respond with a wagging tail and a mutual respect which even I fail to understand.

David has often been criticised for his failure to smile and look as if he is enjoying himself, even when winning some of the highest honours, but those who know him will tell you that no-one takes their dogs more seriously or thinks more of them than he does.

It was while on a trip to the British Utility Breeds Association Championship Show at Bingley Hall, Stafford, in 1983 that David first laid eyes on an Akita. Big Mac of Littlecreek, belonging to Frank and Brett Cassidy, was lying on his bench and from the moment he saw him, David was hooked.

THE GREAT SACHMO

After some research, two bitch puppies were purchased, Overhills Marlows Miracle and Overhills Lizzies Girl, bred by Meg Purnell Carpenter and Sheila

David with Ch. Upend Gallent Ynys whom he handled to his title for Chris and Hazel Culley. *Photo: Dave Freeman.*

Jenny Killilea pictured 'doing the double' with Ch. Rottsann Classic Crusader Of Vormund (Dog CC and BOB) and Dolly Daydream Of Potterspride (Bitch CC) at Belfast Championship Show 1984.

Overhills Marlows Miracle, bred by Meg Purnell-Carpenter, by O'BJ Aces High out of Am. Ch. O'BJ Sachettte No Okii Yubi. A foundation bitch of the Redwitch kennel.

Photo: Hartley.

leading role in the foundation of many kennels in the UK.

The decision to buy was soon seen to be the right one, as the first breeding of McCoy to Miracle produced the first home-bred English Champion Akita bitch, Lizda Zee Zee Flash and Barbados Champion, Lizda Hawaiian Princess. Miracle's sister, Lizzies Girl also played her part by becoming the first Akita to be seen in the Group ring at Crufts, after winning the Not Separately Classified section in 1985. David repeated this win in 1986 with another Sachmo grandson, The Steel Glove O'BJ of Cheney.

We subsequently bred Zee to The Steel Glove and produced what later turned out to be the first Redwitch Champion, Alec and Anne Patterson's Ch. Redwitch Pure Velvet at Tanglemuir.

Gonzalez Camino, out of an import bitch, Am. Ch. O'BJ Sachette No Okii Yubi, and an import dog, O'BJ Aces High, who was subsequently exported to Australia. It was these puppies' grandsire, Am. Ch. Okii Yubi's Sachmo of Makoto, who was to have the greatest impact, and so go on to have the greatest influence on our breeding programme in the future.

Within months, it became apparent that there was not a compatible stud dog in the country, and so the agreement was made to purchase Am. Ch. The Real McCoy O'BJ from B.J. Andrews in the US. McCoy was a Sachmo son and was later to play a

The first American Champion Akita male, and the only Sachmo son to be imported top England. Am. Ch. The Real McCoy O'BJ turned out to be one of the most prolific sires and laid the foundation for many top kennels.
Photo: Hartley.

Ch. Lizda Zee Zee Flash (Am. Ch. The Real McCoy O'BJ – Overhills Marlows Miracle). Bred by David and the first British-bred Champion bitch (handled by Jenny).

Photo: Hartley.

But I digress. While David was showing Bulldogs in Cheshire, I had been showing and breeding another of the bull-breeds, this time Boxers, in Yorkshire. Together with my ex-husband John Dunhill, I then went on to show and breed Rottweilers, under the Vormund affix, with great success and it was through another Rottweiler enthusiast, the late Gordon McNeil, that we were introduced to the Akita.

During the mid-eighties we imported a dog and four bitches from the Hots and Pharfossa Kennels, the most notable of which was another Sachmo grand-daughter, Am. Ch. Hots A Star is Born at Vormund, whom we bred to Vormund Firestorm to produce Ch. Vormund Hot Shot and Nor. Ch. Vormund Hot Stuff.

In 1987 both our marriages were dissolved and David and I formed a new partnership under the Redwitch affix. Even though we had both enjoyed success with the dogs we already owned, decisions now had to be made as to which way the breeding programme was going to go.

It is no secret that we put all our eggs in one basket and line-bred and in-bred to one sire, and were prepared to sink or swim by it. The success has been astounding. The Akita has made us what we are today – the Redwitch affix is known worldwide; but this did not come easily.

INFLUENTIAL IMPORTS
The cost of importing line-bred stud dogs and top-quality brood bitches, plus quarantine fees, put a tremendous strain on our finances and at times even we had to wonder if we were being rational.

In 1988 we purchased Eng. Ch. Goshens Classy Sassy from Julie and Lou Hoehn of Goshen Kennels, Chicago, Illinois. We owe a sincere debt of gratitude to these two people, without whom we would not have enjoyed the success we have had.

We feel we should also mention at this point that the introduction of the Goshen dogs gave us, above all, superb

The 'Queen of Redwitch'. Bought as a brood bitch from the Goshen kennels – and what a superstar she turned out to be! Ch. Goshens Classy Sassy At Redwitch (Am. Ch. Goshen Top Brass – Youtoos Big Busters Babydoll) was the first British Champion bitch.

temperaments which were passed on to their offspring. If you could fault the early dogs it was maybe that they were a little tough, but the Goshen line soon eradicated this.

Sassy proved her worth, not only as a show bitch but instantly as a brood, producing two Champions in her first litter, Dave and Joan Rushby's Ch. Redwitch Secret Affair at Jocolda, the first Akita bitch to win a Reserve Best in Show All Breeds at Championship Show level, and her brother, NZ Ch.

Ch. Am. Ch. Goshens Heir Apparent At Redwitch pictured on his way to becoming the No. 1 Akita in America before joining us at Redwitch. To this date, he is still the top producer of all time in the UK.

Booth Photography.

Redwitch Secret Weapon, owned by Margaret Hippolite, who took his New Zealand title in his first year over there.

Following hot on Sassy's heels came Eng. Am. Ch. Goshens Heir Apparent at Redwitch. Julie and Lou promised to sell him to us as soon as he became America's top Akita and, true to their word, Prince arrived the week after he hit the Number 1 spot.

Even though Prince's achievements were tremendous and his worth as a sire is beyond dispute, the wheel still keeps on turning and two years later we were back in the same position and without a sire for his daughters. Again we had to turn to the Goshen kennels and this time we imported a seven-month-old line-bred male, Eng. Ch. Goshens Dark 'N' Debonaire at Redwitch. Probably the most eye-catching of all our imports, not only for size and substance but for his sheer presence, it was Omar who achieved the pinnacle of our show career by winning Best in Show All Breeds at Manchester Championship Show in 1993.

Ch. Am. Ch. Goshens Heir Apparent At Redwitch. 'Prince' taking his third and crowning ticket at Birmingham 1990 under top all-rounder Jackie Ransom.

To strengthen the line still further we also imported (in conjunction with our great friend, Dr Wayne Welch of Barbados) another bitch, Goshens Hot Wheels, who was a half-sister to Omar, both being sired by Am. Ch. Goshens Chariots O'Fire. She was arrived in-whelp to Am. Ch. Daijobu's Sting of B-Line and the litter was to prove an instant success in the show ring. Ian and Pam MacDonald campaigned Ch. Redwitch Kiss-me-Quick to his title and

Peter Davies followed suit with his first-ever show dog, Ch. Redwitch Kiss 'N' Tell.

At this point we took time to sit back and reflect on what we had achieved. We were producing sound, beautiful Akitas whose type was instantly recognisable. We had won the highest honours in the show ring, from 'the double' at Crufts in the Centenary Year 1991 and Best of Breed again in 1993, to Best in Show All Breeds at Manchester, where we also 'did the double' by winning the qualifying heat of the Spillers/Dog World Pup of the Year Contest with our home-bred puppy Ch. Redwitch Designer Label at her first show. We also qualified the first-ever Akita for the Pedigree Chum Champion Stakes Final. But, in spite of all this, something was missing, and as we could never afford those rose-coloured spectacles, our vision stayed clear – the kennel lacked colour!

So it was back to the drawing-board once more and probably the most testing decision we have had to make. We needed to retain our type and

Ch. Goshens Dark 'N' Debonaire At Redwitch, posing for photographers with Dave in the UK, after our first BIS at Championship show level at Manchester 1993.

Photo: Dave Freeman.

Ch. Goshens Bigger Is Better At Redwitch after taking his first CC. At his very first show, at the tender age of 13 months, under top all-rounder Di Johnson. He went on to take a further 16 CCs.   Photo: John Hartley.

soundness, while introducing a line-bred outcross with colour – our choice was predominantly red.

Once again, Julie and Lou had the perfect answer. Eng. Ch. Goshens Bigger Is Better At Redwitch was a red-and-white male out of the litter sister to Hot Wheels. His sire, however, was a total outcross male who was line-bred back to the famous Tobe Kennel, renowned for their beautiful heads.

Digger, as Bigger Is Better was called,

went on to exceed all our expectations, not only as a show dog, amassing 17 Challenge Certificates, finishing Top Akita 1994 and 1995, Best of Breed at Crufts in 1994 and 1995 and Best Opposite Sex in 1996, but also as a sire, already having produced two Champions, one of which is the bitch breed record holder, and many more top winning progeny. He also finished as Top Sire in 1995 and 1996 and Top Stud Dog in 1996 and 1997.

THE ADVENT OF RAVE

With four generations of prolific males and some top-quality bitches, we have been able to establish a sound foundation for the future. With all we had achieved, it would have been easy to rest on our laurels, but when one of the UK's top all-rounder judges told us we had sold our best abroad, it was like waving a red rag to a bull.

We knew, via interpreters, that Nor. Ch. Redwitch Dancin' in the Dark, then owned by Ola Sukka, had had tremendous success in Norway since being exported by us as a twelve-week-old puppy. It did not take David long to seize the bull by the horns, jump on a plane and secure a deal to bring Rave, as he was known, back to his birthplace.

Six long months in quarantine, followed by a disaster with a trapped nerve in his back, prolonged the efforts to prepare Rave for the competitiveness of the show scene in England. From our previous experience of importing, we knew the stress and strains of bringing out a dog for the first time, but as this one was a re-import that we ourselves had bred, we knew he had to be 101 per cent.

Rave did not let us down. At his very first show in England, Southern Counties in 1996, he took the Dog Challenge Certificate and Best of Breed under top all-rounder Mr Harry Jordan and won the Utility Group under Mr Dennis Coxall. From then on we have not looked back. His title came in three straight shows, and six weeks after his debut, he took his second Group win and Best in Show at East of England Championship Show under Mr Michael Quinney. In 1997, Rave exceeded all our expectations, finishing Top Akita, Top Utility Dog, and Runner-up Top Dog All Breeds, breaking all records with five Best in Shows, one Reserve Best in Show, 10 Group Firsts and 21 Group placements from 23 appearances. His first and only appearance at Crufts 1998 resulted in Best of Breed and a Group 2 placement, with three of his sons standing with him in the final line-up for the Dog Challenge Certificate.

We mentioned earlier that we had line-bred to one particular male. For those of you who have never seen him, it would be difficult to explain the

Ch. Nor. Ch. Redwitch Dancin' In The Dark. 'Rave' seen here taking BIS at Southern Counties 1997 under top American all-rounder, the late Derek Rayne.

Photo: Carol Ann Johnson.

lasting impression Am. Ch. Okii Yubi's Sachmo of Makoto had on us. In Rave, we feel we have achieved a little of the vision that Sachmo left us. Interestingly, in Rave's three-generation pedigree, all but two lines lead directly to Sachmo.

We hope over the next chapters, to share with you some of the knowledge we have gained over the last few years. We do not profess to be experts, only to being lucky enough to have been guided by real experts. Several books have been written on the breed, giving in-depth information on its history and origins. We do intend here also to produce a modern, up-to-date account of the Akita as it is today, to help those coming into the breed, and those who are lucky enough to already own one, in achieving their goal.

Remember, the Red Witch is a learning witch. Even the most knowledgeable of us still has something to learn.

1 ORIGINS OF THE AKITA

The Akita is the largest of the Spitz breeds, which are native to Japan and which share common physical characteristics such as pricked ears, curled tails, and double coats with a harsh outer coat and dense undercoat. The breed was named after its place of origin, the Odate region in Akita Prefecture on the island of Honshu in Northern Japan. Originally called the Odate Dog, this was changed to Akita Inu when the breed was designated by the Japanese as a 'natural monument' in 1931.

Japanese history indicates that it was around the Stone Age that domesticated dogs first appeared in Japan and these were used for hunting and protection. It is not known for certain if these dogs were originally from Japan but it is assumed that the present-day Akita relates back to them. By the Bronze Age, dogs with pricked ears and curled tails and other distinctive features of the Japanese-type dog were to be found, but from then on history is vague and conflicting.

Over the centuries, the different rulers and dignitaries of Japan affected the dog's process of evolution. During the 13th Century, one regent loved dog fighting so much that he collected dogs as taxes from his people. This caused a boom in dog breeding to satisfy the demand for up to 200 dogs fighting each other in a 'free for all' at any one time.

One of the ruling Shoguns, Tsunayoshi, who reigned from 1680 to 1709, decided that as he was born in the Year of the Dog, he would issue a proclamation protecting all living things, especially dogs. It decreed that anyone harming dogs should be executed, so obviously this led to a tremendous stray dog problem. Shelters were built for up to 50,000 dogs which were then cared for at the expense of the taxpayer. One can only wonder at the problems these dogs must have caused, roaming the streets in packs and attacking one another.

Tsunayoshi, who was also known as the Dog Shogun, then established the first dog registry, which not only recorded the size and physical characteristics of the dogs but also the colours, such as red, white, black, brindle and pinto.

During the mid-1800s, along with industrialization, came modernization and the need for raw materials. Fortune hunters from the cities flocked to the countryside in their quest for gold and silver and so, naturally, the crime figures soared. Wealthy farming families now started training their Matagi-Inu, or hunting dogs, as guards, with the emphasis in breeding on size and aggressiveness.

Also at this time, the international maritime trade of Japan was booming and European traders brought with them breeds such as Mastiffs, Great Danes, St Bernards and Bulldogs which were ultimately bred with the Matagi-Inu. As dog fighting was again so popular, the Japanese Tosa was developed and crossbred to produce a fighting machine. Another experimental crossbreeding was with a dog from the formerly Russian islands of Sakhalin. This long-coated dog was known as the Karafuto, a dog with a very calm temperament who was both obedient and eager to please. Today's longcoat

Akitas also very often display these characteristics, so giving credence to the theory that the Karafuto was used in the crossbreeding programme.

And so, eventually, the Akita as we know it today evolved, but it was not until 1931, when the breed was declared a Natural Monument, that this name was used. Even then, the Japanese were not happy with the few dogs which represented the breed, and breeders were cautioned and urged to take greater care with their breeding programmes. Finally, in 1938, the first Akita Dog Standard was written.

HACHI-KO
No history of the Akita would be complete without a mention of the most famous Akita of all – Hachi-Ko.

Hachi-Ko was born in 1923 and belonged to Professor Eizaburo Ueno, a lecturer at Tokyo University. Each morning he accompanied the professor on his walk to Shibuya Train Station and waited each afternoon to

Loyal dog Hachi-Ko in his twilight years.

The monument to Hachi-ko at Shibuya railway station, Tokyo.

accompany him on the walk home. One afternoon, in May 1925, the professor did not return. He had had a fatal stroke while at work. Hachi-Ko waited that night for his master to return and was eventually taken into shelter by friends of the professor. After persistently running away from relatives who tried to care for him and returning each day to the station, Hachi-Ko was eventually fed and cared for by Professor Ueno's gardener. For ten years he continued to wait and mourn for his master and during this time he became a living legend and a national hero.

In 1934 a bronze statue was erected in his honour in front of the Shibuya Station in Tokyo and another near the entrance to the Odate Station in Akita. When he eventually died, on March 8th 1935, a National Day of Mourning was declared. During the Second World War both statues were melted down and used in the war effort, but in 1948 a new one was erected in front of the Shibuya Station and the one at Odate Station was replaced in 1964. They

stand today as a testament to the loyalty and intelligence of the Akita Dog.

THE TRANSITION TO AMERICA
One the first recollections about imports of the Akita into the USA came from the famous author, lecturer and humanitarian, Helen Keller. Miss Keller, who was blind and deaf, was touring Japan in 1937 studying the physically handicapped. After hearing the story of Hachi-Ko, she asked to be introduced to the breed. She was shown a two-month-old puppy belonging to Mr Ogasawara, a member of the Akita area police department, and immediately fell in love with him. His name was Kamikaze-go and Mr Ogasawara agreed to give him to Miss Keller as a present.

When Miss Keller returned to the United States two months later she took Kamikaze-go with her. Unfortunately, within one month, he died from distemper. It was then arranged for Kamikaze's litter brother, Kenzan-go to be shipped to the USA where he quickly became a close friend

16

Black-masked pre-war Akita in his natural environment, where he would have been used for guarding and hunting.

and protector of Miss Keller. She described him as her "Angel in Fur" and he remained with her until his death in the mid-forties.

THE WAR YEARS

This was a very bad time for the Akita in Japan and the breed very nearly became extinct. Because of the food and money shortage, breeders could not afford to feed their dogs and many Akitas were clubbed to death and their beautiful pelts used to keep the military warm. Some owners sent their dogs to remote mountain villages to keep them safe, but even so, few Akitas survived this period.

Fortunately, two things happened which helped to re-establish the breed. The Japanese Government offered help to owners of Champion Akitas if they could not afford to feed them, and interest in the Akita as a Natural Monument was restored. Also the American servicemen in occupied Japan took a tremendous interest in this striking breed. Although it was against the law because there was so few of them, the servicemen started taking their Akitas back home with them to the USA. Breeders in Japan quickly recognised an opening for puppy sales and began farming Akitas, with little regard to quality.

Two particular lines emerged at this time, to which many of today's Akitas can be traced – the Dewa line, whose most famous Akita was Kongo-Go, born in 1947, and the Ichinoseki line, through which came Goromaru-Go in 1948. Dogs from both these lines were imported to the USA, but the Dewa line was most fancied, as the Americans preferred this larger, impressive type of dog.

During the next ten years Akita enthusiasts imported dogs which were to become the foundation stock of today's Akita – both in America and in the UK. Matches and shows were arranged to promote the breed and eventually, on July 13th 1955, the Akita was granted approval by the American Kennel Club to be shown in the Miscellaneous Class at licenced All Breed Shows.

Records show that the first Akitas appearing in competition were at the

Kongo-Go: Born July 1947, a silver sesame from the Dewa line.

The famous Goromaru-Go from the Ichinoseki line. Born in 1948, he was a sesame pinto.

A male Akita born in the 1950s, sired by Kongo-Go out of Asahime-Go.

Kong-Go as a mature male, photographed at around six years of age. he was from the Heirakudo kennel.

Orange Empire Dog Club in San Bernadino, California on January 29th 1956. Five months later, on June 5th 1956, the Akita Kennel Club was formed. This name was changed in 1959 to the Akita Club of America, and its committee had the task of re-writing the Standard of the Breed. As with any committee, there was much divergence of opinion and argument before the newly completed Standard was presented to the AKC in 1964 with a request to transfer the Akita to the working group. This appeal, however, was denied, as the AKC thought that there was not enough cohesion and co-operation between Akita breeders.

Registrations and import figures, however, continued to climb and in October 1972 the breed was finally admitted to AKC registration. On December 12th 1972 approval was given to the Akita Standard based on Japan's Nippo, Akiho and Akikyo Dog Standards. The Akita was admitted to the Working Group on April 4th 1973.

Because all three breed clubs in Japan claimed to be the official governing body and the AKC could not determine which one was correct, in February 1974 they closed the Stud Book and would not allow any further imports from Japan to be registered. At this time 340 import pedigrees were recorded, but of these only 139 were ever used for breeding. From that time until the Stud Book was re-opened in April 1992 no Akitas from Japan were registered.

2 THE AKITA AS A BREED

Your first impression of an Akita should be a lasting one. Nobility, dignity, power, strength, and an awareness of all that is going on around him, make the Akita stand out instantly from the crowd.

Make no mistake, this is a big dog. A fully grown male weighs in at around 110lb and stands approximately 27 inches (69cm) at the shoulder, with the bone and substance to match. But what makes him different from all the rest? It is the large, triangular-shaped head, the broad muzzle, the small pricked ears, the thick, strong neck flowing into a firm back, the powerful rear, the beautiful plush coat in many striking colours and, completing the picture, that unmistakable curled tail, set high and carried firmly over the back. Although this describes the male Akita, we should never underrate the female, who is every bit his equal, but in a slightly reduced package.

Ch. Am. Ch. Goshens Heir Apparent At Redwitch, aged ten years, depicting the strength and nobility of this incredible breed.

We vividly recall the first time we set eyes on the breed and the impact it made on us. Although we already owned strong, impressive breeds, it did not take long before an Akita took pride of place in both of our kennels.

However, appearances can be deceptive. This is a large breed, but the turn of speed and agility of these dogs belies their overall size. While the Akita is normally quite happy to strut around the garden, or trot alongside you for a daily walk, and even run for miles alongside a bike or horse, do not forget that this is also a natural sledge dog – one with the speed of a sprinter and the stamina of a marathon runner.

COLOUR
In many cases, the colour of an Akita is what has originally drawn someone's eye to the breed. There is something here for everyone, whether it be white, black, brindle or pinto, or any shading in between. The plush undercoat, coupled with the harsh outercoat and the stand-off guard hairs, often give a multi-coloured effect: thus a fawn with black overlay can often appear dark silver to the eye. Many people are influenced by the first colour they see and choose a puppy with this in mind.

CHARACTER AND TEMPERAMENT
We are writing this after fifteen years ownership of the breed and even now feel that we are only scratching the surface in understanding the Akita. This is a very complex character with many

A striking dark silver and white puppy – one look and you are hooked.

Photo: Hartley.

Although naturally dominant, this Akita bitch is happy to play with a couple of Cairn Terrier puppies.

contradictions in its personality. In the main, this is a gentle giant who has a very laid-back approach to life. Knowing you are Number One and not having to prove it to anyone gives the Akita that air of authority and calm aloofness so many of us recognize in our dogs. However, do not be misled; the Akita also has a great sense of loyalty and, as your protector, if put in a position where this has to be proven, no questions will be asked.

This is not to say that the breed is an aggressive, going-forward guard dog. For the majority of the time that solemn gaze and arrogant stand is enough to deter any would-be intruder. I am sure anyone who has been met by the black piercing eyes of an Akita they did not know will bear witness to the fact that you would not wish to press the point.

Part of the Akita's character is that it is a reserved and silent breed. Indeed, you will rarely find an Akita barking just for the sake of it. They are normally very quiet, barking only to warn of approaching strangers or to signal something strange or suspicious on their patch.

The Akita should never be nervous, shy or aggressive toward people in normal circumstances – those three characteristics are contrary to the dog's natural instincts. The upbringing and breeding behind an Akita displaying these traits would have to be seriously questioned.

Although not aggressive toward people, the Akita is very dominant over other dogs. While we do not try to encourage this, neither should we seek to alter that which is part of the breed's natural heritage. If you cannot accept this part of an Akita's temperament, then you should consider owning another breed.

Because of the dominance factor, much thought should be given before owning one, or more, of this incredible breed. Obviously, because of their

Little and large: This Akita male has learnt to live side-by-side with his Chihuahua companion.

power and strength, the very elderly or infirm would have great problems controlling these dogs should the need arise. Likewise, it would be very foolhardy to allow a small child to be in charge of an Akita without supervision.

MULTIPLE OWNERSHIP
Two or more Akitas together? Think carefully! While a dog and a bitch will normally run together, without problems, all of their lives, we never recommend anyone buying in a pet situation to have two or more of the same sex. Yes, we can hear the shrieks of horror and the hands held high in amazement by those of you pointing to your beloved pets lying side by side on the couch, but we have also been on the receiving end of countless phone calls and cries for help when two normally friendly females have fallen out over who chased the leaf blowing across the yard, or when the eight-week-old litter brothers, sold by the novice breeder as

inseparables, reached puberty and both decided they wanted to be Number One.

It is possible to have a smaller and more submissive breed live quite happily with an Akita. Indeed, we ourselves have our old Akita bitch, Sassy, or the Queen as she is often referred to, living in the house with a standard, longhaired Dachshund bitch, Tatum, who knows who is the boss and will grovel accordingly, when necessary. Sassy tolerates this impudent young madam, ignoring her for the most part, but occasionally affording her that typical Akita glare when she wanders too close to her feed bowl or tries to muscle in when Sassy herself is having a love and cuddle from ourselves. However, if we need to go out, we always make sure that Tatum is safely ensconced in her bed in the utility room so she cannot pester the old girl, and thus give rise to a problem.

A stunning red/white long-coat Akita – the perfect companion.

THE FAMILY PET

We are often asked if the Akita makes a good pet and, obviously, the answer is yes, they make super pets providing the owner is right. As a house dog, the Akita is spotlessly clean and very easily house-trained. A clever puppy will have learned very early in life which corner of the whelping box to use, so when the pup is introduced to a new home, the right corner of the garden is very soon sought out. This is often the furthest and most remote part the pup can find, as Akitas are a proud and private breed and do not normally like to be watched performing their natural functions. We have spent many hours at showgrounds, walking backwards and forwards with a new show puppy, while he or she finds the spot they are happy with. Then, just when we think it is about to perform, the pup gets up and walks away, only to start the search all over again! Obviously, this trait helps with house-training as the puppy soon learns the perfect spot, and will happily run to it and perform on command.

GROOMING

This is also a scrupulously clean breed, in that an Akita will constantly wash and groom themselves and for this reason they are often referred to as cat-like. The Akita's coat is not hard to look after. It does not normally tangle or mat, and the vacuum cleaner can usually deal with it on a regular basis. However, for the very house-proud among you,

Typical devotion shown by a long-coat Akita.

The well-socialised Akita will accept all types of livestock.

serious thought should be given as to whether you can cope with the twice-yearly 'blow'. When this starts, it is almost like a sheep shedding its coat and daily grooming is required at this time to remove the dead hair as quickly as possible, which in any event can take up to three weeks.

EXERCISE
As far as exercise is concerned, this is very much a dual-purpose dog. For the fitness fanatics, your adult Akita will match you mile for mile, but if your routine only allows for fifteen minutes exercise at either end of the day then this is just as acceptable, with the rest of the time spent happily round the house or garden.

DOMINANCE
As we have already mentioned, this breed is dominant over other dogs and,

while not setting out to look for trouble, the Akita is well capable of dealing with it should it come along. For this reason, great care should always be taken when exercising in public places; you must have your Akita under total control on a lead or flexi-lead.

There is, however, another reason for keeping that lead firmly attached. The inquisitive side of the Akita's nature will always make the far side of the field much more alluring than the path down which you are walking, and your Akita will wave quite happily to you as he or she disappears over the brow of the hill, to return only when every inch of the local countryside has been examined.

TRAINING
One of the most common questions we are asked by would-be owners is "Is the Akita clever and easy to train?" Well, most of the time this dog can out-smart

the best of us. If an Akita will not do something, it is not because it cannot be done, so much as that your dog just does not see the point in doing it. Akitas get bored easily and hate repetition. How many of you, after throwing a ball or stick several times for your Akita to retrieve, have seen the look that says, "You threw it – you fetch it!"

So for this reason, the Akita does not make the best Obedience dog in the world. However, if this is your aim and you still want an Akita, then perhaps consider a long-coat. Possibly because of the ties with the placid Karafuto, the long-coated Akita is generally more eager to please and more biddable than the normal-coated dog and will readily take to Obedience training.

AKITAS WITH CHILDREN

One of the legends associated with the Akita tells how the females were often used as nannies to protect the children in the family while their mothers worked in the rice fields. Indeed there is evidence today that this still may be so in the more remote regions of Japan.

The best of friends, even when it comes to sharing ice-cream.

Akita owners in Japan also send small statues of Akitas as gifts when a baby is born, to ensure a long and healthy life, or as a Get Well Soon gesture when someone is ill. So the breed's association with children has long been known. For those of you with a family, wishing to buy an Akita, this is a super breed to own as a pet and companion, providing you purchase a puppy and you rear both the puppy and your children to have respect for each other.

Growing up together: Mutual respect and tolerance is the key to forming a good relationship.

However, common sense must also prevail and if your house is open to all the neighbourhood kids as well, then think carefully before buying. Shrieking, chasing, unfamiliar youngsters may well arouse the guarding instincts in the Akita who thinks the family children may be being threatened. Likewise, we never recommend anyone with small children to purchase an adult Akita who may never have heard brothers and sisters falling out while playing and may confuse this with threatening behaviour.

AKITAS WITH CATS

As we have mentioned before, the Akita is often referred to as cat-like because of the obsession with cleaning itself, particularly after a meal. The breed also

Above: An Akita brought up with a cat will learn to live in harmony.

An orphan lion cub that was brought up by an Akita, seen here playing with a young dog.

stalks like a cat, silently and low to the ground. However, this does not mean that the two will go together without a problem. Because of the natural hunting trait in the Akita, a fast-moving cat or kitten would often be considered fair prey. So, for this reason, it would be best to bring a puppy and a kitten up together, or introduce a puppy to an adult cat who will soon teach the puppy the rules (providing you watch those sharp claws round puppy's eyes).

The same rules apply in any household where other living creatures are already kept, be it furry or feathered. It is always advisable to start with a puppy, who will quickly learn to respect the other family members and treat them as a normal part of life.

Carol Bevis and Steve Dutton's Ch. Redwitch Prince Consort At Stecal: Runner-up in the Utility Group at the East of England Championship Show 1997, with judge Joe Kirk.

Photo: Hartley.

THE SHOW OR WORKING DOG
Because of the breed's natural stature and glamour, with its many colours and superb coat, the Akita has become a great hit in the show ring, drawing the attention of many eyes. However, a great deal of work and effort is required, both in presentation and training, for those top wins to be possible.

In many cases, the show dog is also a family pet who lives quite happily in the house. However, in a climate where the majority of houses have central heating, this can play havoc with that luxuriant coat. So, if you are thinking of combining the two, the best possible scenario is to have an outside kennel and run, or a totally fenced and secure garden, where your Akita can run out during the day and then spend the evening socializing with the family indoors.

If you must have your dog indoors most of the time, then it is advisable to have somewhere cool as a retreat – a stone or tiled floor, for example – where the dog's belly can be stretched right out, or you will find that that fabulous show coat will blow just as quickly as it came.

This versatile breed makes a natural sledge dog, as we have said, as many proud owners will vouch for. The breed also has several representatives as therapy dogs who do great service for the sick and elderly. Probably the most

Working dogs in harness in Norway.

famous in the UK is Sanjosha's Okusama, or Fuji as she is known, owned by B and Bob Pitts. Fuji is a registered therapy dog with Canine Concern Care and has regularly visited the sick and elderly since 1990. Probably one of her proudest achievements was being instrumental in helping to recover the speech of an elderly stroke victim who had not spoken for over 18 months. Fuji's gentle and trustworthy disposition has made her a great hit both with hospital patients and with the residents of an elderly persons home.

Nor. Ch. Vormund Hot Stuff (foreground), bred by Jenny Killilea, had a successful career in England before being exported to Norway, where most Akitas are dual-purpose.

Fuji's loving disposition has made her a wonderful therapy dog.

3 CHOOSING A PUPPY

Whether you are choosing from your own litter, or purchasing a puppy either for show or as a family pet, you should still basically require the same qualities. You should be looking for an outgoing, friendly puppy with a happy disposition, with substance and size, good bone and a quality coat. Take a look at the ears – they may still be flat on the head at seven to eight weeks, but you should still be able to tell if they will be overly large when the dog is full grown.

Never rush into picking a puppy; they all look good enough to eat at this age, even the really poor ones can melt your heart. Take time to watch them strutting their stuff, playing with their littermates and generally exploring. This will give you a chance to sort out the bold, confident pup from the shy, nervous ones.

CHOOSING A PET
Before dashing out to buy a puppy, you should try to visit a few breeders and meet their fully grown Akitas first to ensure that this is really what you need in your life. If you are a couple, you should both go together, as it is no good one of you wanting a strong, male Akita if your other half cannot cope.

You will possibly have been attracted to the breed by the many variations in colour. If this is true and you have one colour in mind, then wait for that

Jenny with a typical Redwitch puppy. Taking on a big powerful breed such as the Akita is a major commitment.

Photo: Hartley.

29

Akita puppies have a charm of their own, but you must try to be objective when making your choice. This puppy became a Champion in the show ring. Photo: Hartley.

special puppy as, hopefully, it will be with you for a long time and if you settle for a second choice, you may be disappointed later.

Temperament must be first and foremost in a family pet and to this end you should ask to see either or both of the parents if possible. Although this does not guarantee good temperament, it should give you some idea and peace of mind. You should also enquire as to the hip status of both parents and if they have clear eye certificates. Again this is no guarantee, but it gives your puppy the best start possible and also proves that you have chosen a caring breeder.

MALE OR FEMALE

Many people are drawn to males by their sheer size and substance, but you should seriously consider whether all the family can cope. Although very often the husband wants a male, it is often left to the wife to look after the dog and if she feels that she cannot physically deal with a dog of this size, it will only lead to problems. In this case, a bitch is equally good, but in a smaller package. Bitches can also be slightly more loving and family-orientated, while the dog often remains more aloof and territorial. On the down side, bitches come into season every six months and this has to be coped with, but they can be spayed later on and this then removes the problem without any ill effects.

FINDING A BREEDER

There are various ways of finding reputable breeders. Your national Kennel Club will have a list of people from all areas of the country and gladly pass this information on. It can also put you in touch with the breed club secretaries who can also help with names of Akita breeders in your area. Dog shows are also a good way to establish contact, and in the UK, for example, the Kennel Club runs a "Discover Dogs" at Crufts Dog Show and one at Earls Court once a year where all breeds are on show and information can be gathered.

There is a wide range of monthly and

weekly magazines all aimed at the dog enthusiast and many contain advertisements and information about Akita breeders. They also contain dates and times of all forthcoming shows and most top breeders will be found at the general Championship shows. Without doubt, the most recent innovation on offer is the Internet, which not only gives you access to breeders but also allows you to talk to enthusiasts all over the world.

THE SHOW PROSPECT

Having studied the pedigrees and visited various breeders, you have finally found the litter you have been looking for. So how do you pick that special puppy and what should you be looking for? While looking at the whole of the litter, you should instantly recognise among the puppies the extrovert, the showman, or showgirl, the puppy with confidence not only in what he does, but in the way he carries himself. Take a long look at the shape and outline, the

ASSESSING SHOW POTENTIAL

Left: Icibans Hachimitsu-Go aged six weeks. Note the front, the topline, the tail-set and coat quality of this lovely puppy, owned by Loren and Christina Egland.

Right: The ears should be small, thick, and rounded at the tip.

Left: A beautiful picture of Ch. Koma-Inu Keep On Bruin, bred by Judythe Dunn. At nine weeks of age, this pup is already showing superb bone and substance, a fabulous head (although the ears are not yet erect), and quality throughout.

AKITA COLOURS

There is something for everyone in the many striking colours of the Akita. From pure white, through shades of fawn, red, silver and black, to the attractively marked brindles, you are bound to find something which catches your eye.

White.

Red and White.

Fawn and White.

Two Red and Whites.

Silver and White Pinto.

Silver Brindle.

Silver/Black overlay and White.

Black Brindle.

FULFILLING POTENTIAL

Am. Ch. Daijobu's Joto (aged six months), owned and bred by Catherine and Charles Bell.

Am. Ch. Daijobu's Joto now fully mature.
Photo: Bernard W. Kernan.

way he carries his neck and ears and his tail carriage. What you see now at seven weeks should basically be the shape and outline that the dog will finish with when fully mature. If he does not have angulation at this age, he never will.

Stand the puppy on a table and see how he or she stacks up. Take a look at the width of chest – are both front legs 'coming out of the same hole' i.e. too close together? If they are, the front will never be correct. Examine the head. Is there a well-defined stop? If not, the puppy will finish with a weak, untypical head and expression. Check the colour of the eyes and that they are dry with no sign of any eye problem. Examine the ears: they should be small, thick and

rounded at the tip. If there is no strength of muzzle now, it will not come later; and take a very good look at the teeth – the bite is so important in an Akita. Although these are the milk teeth and the pup will lose these later, you can still get a good indication of how the bite will finish.

If you are purchasing a male puppy, you need to check if he has two testicles. Although at seven to eight weeks they may not necessarily be descended, as Akitas can often be late developing in this department, it is wise to check, and you should at least be able to find them by around twelve to thirteen weeks. Something else to check is the quality of coat the puppy is carrying. Even at this tender age, a puppy should carry a full, stand-off coat; if it is flat and short now, chances are it always will be.

Now put the puppy down on the floor and give him some space to trot around. Watch how he moves at the front and the rear and that he is not doing anything untoward with his legs. If you were in any doubt about whether he was out at the elbow while on the table, you should be able to confirm this now by carefully watching the front movement as puppy comes towards you. A good puppy will usually stand four-square quite naturally when something catches his attention, and as the saying goes, 'if he's built right, he will usually move right'; but there are, however, always the exceptions to the rule.

If you have cut your selection down to two or even three pups, which all seem to be of equal quality, the deciding factor should then be colour and markings. As you are intending to be able to show this puppy, the one with flashy, striking markings will stand out in the crowd. However, be wary of markings which will detract from the dog's expression, for example a white blaze which runs to one side of the face, particularly if it covers one eye, as this can give a very odd expression. Also, leg markings can be deceptive. Uneven markings on one rear leg can give the appearance that the dog is not moving correctly; so where possible, choose a puppy with balanced markings.

One final point as regards to choosing a show puppy. We are often asked whether we are keeping a dog or a bitch from our latest litter which may have just been born. Our answer is always the same, 'We are keeping the best puppy.' We never decide beforehand that we will keep one sex or the other, we always wait to see which is the most outstanding; that way we are never disappointed.

ARRIVING HOME
Having made the big decision and finally made your choice, the big day

Your puppy will feel bewildered when he first arrives in his new home.

arrives when you can at last bring your puppy home. Even before arriving home, the way the pup reacts to travelling will give you some indication as to his attitude to life. While the odd nervous or introvert puppy will sit with 'candles' drooling from either side of the mouth, most Akita pups will take this new adventure in their stride and tumble out of the car at the other end with the look that says 'I've arrived'.

It is important to make this first journey as stress-free as possible, as Akita puppies have incredible memories and if you intend showing or just having a permanent companion, you need a happy traveller.

You should have already decided on the sleeping accommodation and whether your puppy will live in the house or have a kennel and run outside. If it is your intention to have the puppy permanently living in, then you must have some sort of bed or basket, preferably in a corner where the puppy can feel secure and sleep undisturbed for those important first growing weeks. It is not advisable to give a pup of this age the whole run of the house. Apart from the fact that your best pair of shoes, or the edge of the new kitchen unit, will be far more alluring than that chew bone you just bought, there are many dangers lurking out there which puppies should not be exposed to. Up and down stairs and on and off the couch are definite no taboos. Akita puppies have tremendous bone and, at this age, lack the muscle to support it, so what appears to be just a small jump from the easy chair can do untold damage to shoulder or hip joints.

For those occasions when you cannot be there to supervise, or for safety overnight, a large cage or puppy pen is an ideal solution. It will give you peace

Allow your puppy a chance to explore the garden.

of mind, and at the same time afford the puppy a measure of security, knowing that while he is in it, no small members of the family can torment him or disturb his sleep.

HOUSE TRAINING

Having a cage can also help with that other puppy problem – house training. Akitas are by nature a very clean breed, so most puppies will not wish to soil their bed area. Providing you take your puppy outside for regular visits, you will find that he – or she – will very quickly learn to relieve himself on command. Immediately after feeding or upon awakening from sleep, you should take puppy outside and always give the same command. You will be amazed at how soon a young Akita will decide which is the most private and suitable part of the garden and will return there time after time to perform his duty. Although some people prefer to train to newspaper first, we find that as long as you are prepared to put the work in for a couple of weeks, an Akita puppy will house train very easily, as this is a naturally clean breed.

If you have decided to keep your puppy in an outside kennel and run, you will realise immediately how clean the breed is, as puppy will return to the same spot day after day. In this case, you should regularly use a good-quality disinfectant and odour eliminator to keep the ground germ-free and smelling fresh. It is also important that you clean up after your puppy in the garden as, apart from the hygiene aspect, he will not wish to return to a badly soiled area.

FEEDING AND EXERCISE

Whatever food your puppy was reared on by the breeder, you should arrange to bring some home with you, so you do not change the diet as well as the environment. This way, if puppy is upset or has loose motions for a day or two, you can eliminate change in diet as the problem. Whether you decide to feed a complete food or a regular biscuit with meat, it is important for puppy to have a routine and have regular feeding times. Remember, over-feeding can be just as damaging as under-feeding, so try to strike a happy medium.

Akita puppies should never be exercised, that is put on a lead and taken for long walks. Given the chance, they will exercise themselves quite happily around the house and garden and when tired will flop down and survey their world. You should slowly start to build the exercise up – and this not until the puppy is well grown and over six months old.

TRAINING AND SOCIALIZATION

Although your puppy does not need exercise, socializing is a must. It is a good idea to get your puppy used to a collar for a few days before attempting to attach a lead. For this you will need a little patience and understanding, as you

Training and socialisation should start from day one.

could get anything from a double somersault to a back-flip. However, with a little coaxing and maybe the help of a few tidbits, puppy should soon learn to trot happily on a lead.

Now you can start the socializing process. An Akita needs to be introduced to other dogs and animals from an early age so that they become a normal part of life and not a challenge to be taken up. Take puppy to the local park in the car and let him or her sit and watch life going by. You are not there to exercise your puppy, but to introduce him to all aspects of life, whether it be people, dogs, cats or traffic. This is an essential part of growing up and, done correctly, will lead to a well-balanced, well-mannered Akita puppy. It is at this age that your puppy should learn right from wrong and should be taught to respect you and understand that you are the pack leader. Never allow an Akita to dominate you and to do something against your wishes. Your puppy will quickly recognise the weakness and treat you as an inferior. The training you put in now will be reflected later on in life when, as a headstrong teenager, your Akita may think twice before doing as you bid. If your training has been correct, he or she will not think a third time.

Given a little luck and a lot of patience, you will end up with one of the best friends and companions you could ever wish for and, unlike human friends, an Akita will never, ever, let you down.

4 CARING FOR YOUR AKITA

To ensure that your Akita reaches maturity in good health and has developed correctly, you must make sure that you provide a diet which meets the nutritional needs of your dog. Age, activity level and climate are all important factors in determining which type of food is required.

NUTRITION AND FEEDING

Akita puppies grow at an incredible rate so they need a food high in top-quality proteins with added vitamins, minerals and calcium, and a higher fat level, to ensure maximum growth. However, beware of overfeeding your Akita puppy; fat is not beautiful and an obese puppy can later suffer from both structural and muscular problems due to unnecessary strains on those growing joints.

Once maturity has been reached, a lower protein and fat level should be fed, particularly if your Akita is just a family pet whose maximum amount of exercise is a run in the local park every evening. However, in times of stress, such as when a bitch is lactating, higher protein is again required, as it is for a working stud dog who needs to be kept in top condition. Akitas which live in a kennel situation all year round may need a higher protein and fat content during really cold winter months to ensure they retain correct body weight.

In the veteran dog, weight gain can sometimes be a problem due to a slower metabolism or decreased activity. On the other hand, at this time, absorption or digestive problems may occur, making it difficult to maintain weight. A close eye should be kept on your Akita during the twilight years and a top-quality food given, though one not high in protein or fat, in order to ensure that your friend is with you for as long as possible.

DOG FOODS

There are different schools of thought

GROWTH RATE

*The growth rate of an Akita puppy is phenomenal. Here we follow Redwitch Strike Up
The Band For Silverhawk, owned by Sue and Ian Johnson, from two days to 12 months.*

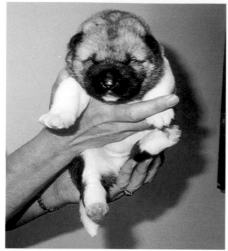

Two days old.

Ten weeks.

Four weeks.

Six months.

Seven weeks.

Twelve months.
Photo: Carol Ann Johnson.

about how to feed dogs and many people still use, very successfully, fresh meat or tripe and biscuits. However, others feed a complete extruded food and have had excellent results from this.

With the vast range of feeds available, you should study the labels carefully to ensure you purchase a food catering for the correct nutritional needs of your Akita. Many of the foods sold in the supermarkets are not extruded but of the 'expandable' nature. These are not suitable for Akitas as they can cause gas and bloating. If you are unsure, drop a few pieces of your dog food into a glass containing water and leave it to soak for about an hour. If it is expandable food, it will have doubled in size, whereas the extruded food will have only softened and slightly increased. Also, a good-quality extruded food will not have broken into pieces, but will still be completely formed when soaked.

These top-quality extruded foods contain only meat or poultry meal as their source of protein and not by-products or soya. Because of this they are more easily absorbed and digested, so smaller amounts provide more nutrition. This also leads to less waste coming out of the other end, another very acceptable reason for feeding an extruded food!

One of the most recent innovations on the dog food market is the lamb and rice or chicken and rice meal, and we have found that this is usually excellent when Akitas are suffering from dietary problems, sensitive stomachs or colitis, resulting in much improved, properly formed motions. Because of their easy digestibility, they also help with weight gain.

We always damp the food down by the addition of a cup of warm water – if for no other reason than that, as all our Akitas are exceptionally good eaters, it stops the kibble from bouncing back out of the bowl as the dog's head goes in. However, it does also help to bring out the smell and make the food more appealing. It goes without saying that clean, fresh water should always be available.

SUPPLEMENTS
We are often asked if canned meat or leftovers can be safely added to a complete diet, or if they need a supplement of calcium or vitamins. Most of the top-quality feeds have been specially formulated to give your dog a balanced diet containing all the vitamins and minerals that are required. By adding to them, in particular with fresh, high-protein meat, you risk unbalancing the formula. However, a spoonful of canned meat, tripe or fresh vegetables will help to give 'smell' appeal to the fussy eater and will do no harm, providing it is kept in moderation.

The addition of calcium is something we do not normally recommend when a complete food is being fed, as problems such as osteochondrosis dissecans may be attributed to the oversupplementation of this and, as previously mentioned, calcium is already contained in the food. However, there are certain supplements on the market which can be added to the food to help in times of stress – for instance, with in-whelp bitches, lactating mothers or with a dog blowing its coat, providing the instructions are carefully read and adhered to. If in doubt, always consult your vet first.

SNACKS AND TREATS

There are various treats on the market which will satisfy your Akita's need to chew, while at the same time cleaning the teeth and exercising the gums. Opinion is often divided on whether to give bones or not, but if you do, only give the large knuckle bones which will not splinter. These can now be purchased already roasted and most Akitas go crazy for them. Other favourites are pigs' ears and cows' hoofs.

EXERCISE

Without doubt, the first rule about exercise is *never* immediately following a meal, as this can drastically increase the tendency to bloat.

From puppyhood to veteran, all Akitas love exercise whether it be just fifteen minutes or as much as two hours daily, and if you cannot afford to spend this time enjoying it with your dog, you should not own one. As with children, this is the quality time, spent bonding

Ch. Keskai First Love bred by Sue and Kevin Sadler, owned by Carl and Shirley Jones. It is important to guard against over-exercising youngsters during the vital growing period.

with your dog, watching your Akita enjoying life.

As previously mentioned, puppies need little in the form of real exercise, save what they do themselves racing round the garden. While the bones are still soft and the muscles not yet formed, road work is a no-no. However, they must be allowed some freedom and let out to play regularly or they will soon become too fat and lethargic, which will lead to problems later on.

Once your Akita reaches eight or nine months, you can begin to exercise, preferably on soft ground which will not jar the joints, and then slowly increase both distance and duration. Once the bone growth is completed, road work can be undertaken, which will help to build muscle. As an adult, your Akita can take as little or as much exercise as you can give. This is the time when you and your dog can both enjoy life while, at the same time, realising the benefits exercise can give. For the fitness fanatics jogging, or even cycling, with your Akita can be great fun, while those of you who are less adventurous can enjoy a stroll in the countryside or the local park. You should soon learn the correct amount of time which it is necessary to spend exercising in order to keep your dog trim and healthy – and you will be amazed at what it can do for your own figure too!

While on the subject of exercise, you should make sure that your Akita is always equipped in a correctly fitting collar suitable for the power of an Akita, together with an identification tag and a lead or flexi-lead to match. When people or other dogs are about, your Akita should always be under complete control and on a lead, no matter how obedient. Even the best-natured Akita will not back down from the threats of a stray dog.

Swimming is another excellent form of exercise and is brilliant for muscle toning. However, although most Akitas can and will swim, it is not something that most will do for fun or take to readily. It can also play havoc with that luxuriant coat, especially in chlorine-

The adult Akita will enjoy and benefit from the exercise he is given.

treated water, so if you are swimming for health reasons, to rehabilitate an injured dog for instance, then expect the coat to blow or to need conditioning afterwards.

COMMON AILMENTS
As a breed, the Akita is generally very healthy and hardy and, with good upbringing, will live a long and trouble-free life. However, one of the breed's downfalls is its very high pain threshold, so by the time you realise something is amiss, your Akita may be very ill. Prevention is always better than cure, so start as you mean to go on by making sure that your puppy is vaccinated against the common ailments – distemper, hepatitis, leptospirosis, parvovirus and parainfluenza. These

Redwitch War Lord, owned by Anne and Alec Patterson.
The Akita is a hardy breed and, with the correct care, should experience few health problems.

Photo: Michael Trafford.

diseases are being seen less and less because of the success of modern immunization programmes, but we should not become complacent and should have puppies vaccinated twice and then given an annual booster. We inject at eight weeks and then twelve weeks, but different vets have different routines and you should always consult your own vet to establish when he will want to see your puppy. Apart from protecting your dog from illness, these injections are also necessary if you ever wish to use the services of a boarding kennel, as most reputable establishments will require these to be up to date, and a certificate produced on arrival.

Kennel cough is another common ailment which is not breed specific. This virus is airborne and can be transferred from one dog to another anywhere from the local park to your last visit to a dog show. Again it can be vaccinated against, and while in mature, otherwise healthy dogs it can be nothing more than an irritation, for young stock or the elderly it can be very severe or even life-threatening.

Although the UK is currently rabies-free, many other countries, including the USA, have mandatory laws requiring all dogs to be vaccinated against this disease. The rabies virus is contracted when broken skin or mucous membranes come into contact with the saliva of a contaminated animal, and is contagious through contact with humans and other animals. The rabies vaccine is not normally given until after the dog is four months old. All dogs entering the UK are automatically vaccinated against rabies on entering quarantine.

You may wish to consider having your Akita micro-chipped or tattooed. In the event of the dog being lost or wandering off, you are then safe in the knowledge that your pet can be easily identified and returned to you.

WORMING

The most common type of worm found in dogs is the roundworm. These worms migrate from the in-whelp bitch to the developing foetus, or are passed to the young by the lactating bitch. Easily identifiable symptoms are pot-bellies, dull coat and lack of condition, lack of growth and coughing which is caused by the worms migrating through the lungs. Badly infested puppies can also vomit up worms. Thorough worming of the bitch prior to breeding can drastically reduce the incidence of roundworm in the puppies, but these can be safely treated with several very good types of worm medications available from your vet. Puppies should be wormed at the direction of your vet with the medication he or she provides. This is especially important in households where there are small children, as the worm eggs are passed in the infected dog's motions and remain viable for some time in the soil. The larvae can then migrate to children if soil is ingested which is contaminated with roundworm eggs.

Tapeworm also infests dogs, especially in insanitary conditions. Symptoms are normally an increased appetite coupled with weight and condition loss. Rice-like grains appear in the motions and can sometimes be seen round the dog's anus. Again your vet can provide you with effective medication.

Heartworm is not normally a problem in the UK, but it is being seen increasingly in the USA. Heartworms are transmitted from dog to dog by mosquitoes; the worms live and grow in the bloodstream, lodging in the heart and lungs. Symptoms include coughing, breathing difficulties and weakness, but often these signs go unnoticed until the condition is advanced. Preventative medicines can now be given, provided the dog is certified clear of heartworm in the first place. Dogs coming into the UK from overseas should be checked for heartworm.

FLEAS AND TICKS

The bane of all dog owners' lives, to which there is no easy solution, is the problem of fleas, which can be picked up by the cleanest of dogs from grasses, bushes, from wildlife or even the neighbourhood cat, particularly in warm weather or after a very dry spell. There are many different types of sprays and shampoos on the market, some of which seem to work and some of which don't. Probably one of the most effective remedies currently available are those new drops which are placed behind the neck around the withers and which can be effective for up to three months. They are available from most vets. However, you must not forget to cleanse thoroughly your Akita's sleeping quarters, bedding and any carpets which may also harbour these little visitors!

Ticks can be picked up by your dog while out walking in the countryside, particularly where sheep are about. If your Akita is unlucky enough to collect one of these parasites, do not try to pull it off, as you will leave the head embedded, so causing irritation and possible infection. First soak the tick in alcohol and wait for it to release its grip, then remove it with tweezers. Ticks should be carefully disposed of by either burning them or flushing them down the toilet.

BLOCKED ANAL GLANDS

If your Akita persistently starts to chase his tail or drags his rear along the ground when in the sitting position, the chances are that blocked anal glands are the problem.

This is easily remedied with a quick trip to the vet who can clear the blocked passages in seconds.

PRESSURE POINTS

How many times have you given your Akita a nice new fleece or blanket to lie on, only to return ten minutes later to see it shredded into two-inch squares? As a breed they seem to enjoy lying stretched out on cold concrete, so it is probably no surprise that they can be prone to pressure sores on hocks and elbows. On white legs this also discolours the coat as well as damaging hair growth. A topical lubricant applied to the pressure points may help to prevent this, and an antibiotic cream should be used should bleeding or soreness occur.

SORE TESTICLES

Similarly, the testicles on male Akitas can be affected by constant rubbing on concrete or even nylon carpets. This can lead to more severe problems if ignored, resulting in the dog becoming temporarily or permanently sterile. Sore patches should be treated immediately with antiseptic cream and a course of antibiotics.

FROZEN TAIL

This is a peculiar phenomenon in the Akita which no-one seems to have an explanation for but which seems to occur after bathing. The nerves in the root of the tail seem to be affected and this makes the tail drop from its normal position. The tail can remain in this down position for anything from three to four days to as long as two weeks and it will be very sensitive during this time. There is no easy answer as to why it happens, and there does not appear to be any cure; only time will rectify it. It is best to leave the tail alone during this period, as prodding and poking only seem to antagonise the dog further. After experiencing this on a couple of occasions with our own dogs, we are now ultra-careful when bathing, trying not to remove the tail off the back, but washing it while it is in the natural position.

POPPING HOCKS

This is the description for a weak hock joint which, when pushed from the rear will 'pop' through to give a double-jointed appearance, more commonly seen together with a straight stifle. This not only looks unsightly, but denotes weak construction – not desirable in a dog with the strength and substance of an Akita.

DOG FIGHTS

While we all recognise the dominance factor in our breed and take precautions accordingly, occasionally accidents do happen and two dogs get together. If you are unfortunate enough to have this happen to you, do not rush in and grab hold. Fighting dogs do not recognise that a stray arm belongs to their master and friend and you could find yourself on the receiving end of a nasty bite, albeit unintentional. If you are lucky, because of the thickness of the Akita coat, the only damage may be mouthfuls of hair. On the other hand, a serious fight can result in deep puncture wounds, lacerations or even torn-off ears, in which case the vet's advice should be sought as to whether antibiotics are needed as well as treatment for any damage.

BLOAT

This is a condition which afflicts most large breeds, including the Akita. Fortunately it is not common, but unfortunately it can be extremely serious, quite often resulting in death. It is usually caused by gases from food being released into the stomach, causing it to swell and, in severe cases, to twist. If this happens, the gases cannot be released, pressure is put on body organs, nerves and blood supplies are compressed and this results in shock and death. Symptoms to watch for are the stomach swelling rapidly and becoming hard, severe discomfort, attempts to vomit and defecate and drooling. Should these occur, time is of the essence and you should rush your Akita to the vet immediately, forewarning him or her of your impending arrival.

Quite often, dogs surviving the operation unfortunately cannot cope with the post-operative shock, although Akitas have been known to survive both. However, owners should be aware that the condition can re-occur and often within a few days. Suggested precautions are never exercising immediately prior to feeding, or immediately afterwards, and giving two smaller meals per day rather than one large meal.

INTUSSUSCEPTION

A problem which occurred more frequently in the early days of the breed, and fortunately seemingly not as common these days. It occurs when sections of the intestine concertina into themselves and it is more commonly seen in puppies. First symptoms are the puppy sitting in a corner on its own, away from its litter mates, vomiting and having gravy-like diarrhoea, sometimes containing blood. If the condition is recognised quickly enough, the intestine can be tacked down or sections removed and the puppy can live a normal, long and happy life. We have had puppies as young as five weeks survive this operation and go on to be normal, healthy Akitas. Indeed, in the case of one bitch puppy, she later produced a litter containing one of the top bitches in this country.

POISONING
Puppies have a higher chance of being poisoned than have adult dogs because of their mischievousness and curiosity. However, exercising your Akita down country lanes can also be a hazard when farmers have sprayed their crops with pesticides. Other poisons which rapidly spring to mind as being easily obtained by your dog are slug pellets, rat poison, weed killers or even toadstools or laburnum seeds. As with children, watch your Akita's play areas and if

poisoning is suspected, take your dog immediately to the vet together with, where possible, a sample of the offending substance.

DIARRHOEA
This can be caused by a variety of reasons from severe gastro-enteritis needing immediate veterinary advice, to an overly excited dog. Other common causes are over-feeding, a change of diet or even stress. Diarrhoea causes dehydration, so make sure your dog has fresh water available, but withhold food for twenty-four hours and allow the stomach to rest. After a severe bout of diarrhoea, we often give natural live yoghurt which replaces the food-digesting bacteria which have been stripped from the intestines. A lighter diet of boiled rice and fish or chicken, or scrambled or boiled eggs, should then be offered, but if symptoms persist, your vet's advice should be sought.

5 THE AKITA STANDARD

The Standard is the most important thing you will need to know as an enthusiast, as a breeder, or as a judge. It should be stamped in your head as a blueprint for the breed and remain there as a point of reference at any time. It was written many years before we set eyes on this incredible breed and will remain there for many years after we are gone. We are only the guardians for the short time that we are privileged to be involved with the Akita, and as such we should strive to preserve the breed in its true form and not try to alter it to suit modern trends or fads.

Although the Akita type as we know it may have changed over the years, we must start with the standard of the country of origin – the Japanese Standard, which is also the Standard of the Fédération Cynologique Internationale (FCI). In Japan, there have always been several different Akita Clubs, the Nippo being the first to be formed in 1923, followed by the Akiho in 1924, and later the Akikyo in 1943. However, the Japan Kennel Club is the governing body overseeing all breeds and working closely with the FCI, and it was through them that the decision to withhold top awards from the 'American type' came.

THE FCI STANDARD
Through the 1980s and early 1990s the pure Japanese type, the pure American type and crossbreedings between the two were all shown in the same ring on the Continent. The black-masked dog of the American/British type took many top honours, from Championship title to Best in Show. With the friction between the two types coming to the fore in the mid-1990s, a decision was taken by the FCI to accept only the Standard of the country of origin, thereby effectively disqualifying the black-masked dog from top honours.

This, without doubt, caused more

friction, as many enthusiasts had spent 10 to 15 years improving the American/British type, showing and breeding very successfully. The ruling left them with the right to breed their dogs and the right to show them, but only the right to win, at best a second prize, no matter what the quality of the opposition.

In late 1997 and in 1998 we have seen a big push by the owners of this type of Akita, and also with the backing of some European Kennel Clubs, to split the breed and regain recognition for the American/British type. It would appear that the best solution would be a natural split, with no cross-breeding between the two, thus preserving the quality in standard of both types. Obviously, no matter what the

outcome, there will be those who disagree with the decision. However, this way, both types will be preserved and be capable of competing in fair competition, neither being detrimental to the other.

Although we, personally, have been extremely successful with the American type, we also have tremendous respect for, and admire greatly, the Japanese Akita. We do not know what the future holds, but it is not difficult to envisage that, one day, the Redwitch kennel, among others, could quite happily run both types alongside each other, while retaining the purity of each.

THE OFFICIAL FCI STANDARD
ORIGIN: Japan

DATE OF PUBLICATION OF THE ORIGINAL VALID STANDARD: 01.01.1998

UTILIZATION: Companion dog.

CLASSIFICATION FCI: Group 5 Spitz and primitive type.
   Section 5 Asian Spitz and related breeds.

Without working trial.

BRIEF HISTORICAL SUMMARY
Originally Japanese dogs were small to medium in size and no large breeds existed. Originating in the Tohoku Area, as a hunting dog of

A typical 'Japanese' Akita, owned by Pat Szymanski, being shown Japanese style.

medium size as an "Akita Matagi" (bearhunting dog), around 1630-1679 under the Stake Clan in the Akita region, breeding of the breed to promote dog fights was encouraged in order to raise the moral of the land barons in the region, according to remaining historical records. Subsequently the breed was cross bred with the dog thought to be a Mastiff owned by the German mining engineer at the Kosaka copper mine and with a Tosa fighting dog (cross bred from the medium-sized Japanese breed Shikoku Mastiff crossed with German Pointers, St. Bernards and Great Danes, etc.); the heretofore known identity of pointed ears and ringtails which were originally characteristic of Akitas was lost. In 1908 dog fighting became prohibited and public opinion gradually favoured preserving this breed among professors and learned people. In 1919 the law for preservation of natural monuments was established, and as a result of fanciers' efforts to improve the breed thereafter, in 1931 nine superior dogs of this breed was designated as natural monuments, and the breed became widely popular. At the end of the 2nd World War in 1945, efforts were made to eliminate the strain of the Mastiffs and other foreign breeds from the few remaining Akitas to establish a pure Akita and succeeded in stabilizing the pure strain of large Akitas known today.

GENERAL APPEARANCE Large-sized dog sturdily built, well balanced and with much substance, secondary sex characteristics strongly marked, with high nobility and dignity in modesty; constitution tough.

IMPORTANT PROPORTIONS The ratio of height at withers to length of body (from the point of the shoulders to the point of the buttock) is 10:11, but the body is slightly longer in bitches than in dogs.

BEHAVIOUR AND TEMPERAMENT: The temperament is composed, faithful, docile and receptive.

HEAD
CRANIAL REGION
Skull: The size of the skull is in proportion to the body. The forehead is broad, with distinct furrow. No wrinkle.
Stop: Defined.

FACIAL REGION
Nose: Large and black. In case of white coat, flesh colour permitted.
Muzzle: Moderately long and strong with broad base, tapering but not pointed. Nasal bridge straight.

Jaws/Teeth: Teeth strong with scissor bite.
Lips: Tight.
Cheeks: Moderately developed.
Eyes: Relatively small, almost triangular in shape due to the rising of the outer eye corner, set moderately apart, dark brown; the darker the better.
Ears: Relatively small, thick, triangular, slightly rounded at tips, set moderately apart, pricked and inclining forward.

NECK Thick and muscular, without dewlap, in balance with head.

BODY
Back: Straight and strong.
Loin: Broad and muscular.
Chest: Deep, forechest well-developed, ribs moderately well sprung.
Belly: well drawn up.

TAIL Set on high, thick, carried vigorously curled over back; the tip nearly reaching hocks when let down.

LIMBS
FOREQUARTERS
Shoulders: moderately sloping and developed.
Elbows : Tight.
Forearms: straight and heavy-boned.

HINDQUARTERS Hindlegs well developed, strong and moderately angulated.

FEET Thick, round, arched and tight.

GAIT Resilient and powerful movement.

COAT
HAIR Outer coat harsh and straight, undercoat soft and dense; the withers and the rump are covered with slightly longer hair; the hair on tail is longer than on the rest of the body.

COLOUR Red fawn, sesame (red fawn hairs with black tips), brindle and white. All the afore-mentioned colours except white must have URAJIRO. (URAJIRO – whitish coat on the sides of the muzzle, on the cheeks, on the underside of jaw, neck, chest, body and tail and on the inside of the legs.)

SIZE Height at withers: dogs, 67cms; bitches, 61cms. There is a tolerance of 3cms more or less.

FAULTS Any departure from the foregoing points should be considered a fault and the seriousness with which the fault should be regarded should be in exact proportion to its degree.
Bitchy dogs / Doggy bitches.
Undershot or overshot mouth.

18-24 MOS
DOG
SWEEPSTAKES
AKITA
CLUB OF AMERICA

Am. Ch. Bogarts Playin' For Keeps, with owner/handler Paula Ebner. An excellent example of the 'American' Akita, oozing breed type.

Photo: Alverson.

Missing teeth.
Spotted tongue.
Iris light in colour.
Short tail.
Black mask.
Markings on white background.
Shyness.

DISQUALIFYING FAULTS
Ears not pricked.
Hanging tail.
Long hair (shaggy).

NB: Male animals should have two apparently normal testicles descended into the scrotum.

THE AMERICAN STANDARD

This Standard was approved by the American Kennel Club in April 1973. As with many breeds, there have been several earlier interpretations, but after much discussion and deliberation on the part of the committee, during which several notable divergences from the FCI Standard were introduced, the final outcome was the AKC Standard as we know it today. However, these differences could be one of the underlying reasons behind the fact that the Akita in the USA and in Japan has developed in different ways with two distinctive types emerging.

THE OFFICIAL AKC STANDARD

GENERAL APPEARANCE Large, powerful, alert, with much substance and heavy bone. The broad head, forming a blunt triangle, with deep muzzle, small eyes and erect ears carried forward in line with the back of neck, is characteristic of the breed. The large, curled tail, balancing the broad head is also characteristic of the breed.

HEAD Massive but in balance with body, free of wrinkle when at ease. Skull flat between ears and broad; jaws square and powerful with minimal dewlap. Head forms a blunt triangle when viewed from above. Fault: Narrow or snipy head.

MUZZLE Broad and full. Distance from nose to stop is to distance from stop to occiput as 2 is to 3.

STOP Well defined, but not too abrupt. A shallow furrow extends well up forehead.

NOSE Broad and black. Liver permitted on white Akitas, but black always preferred.
Disqualification: Butterfly nose or total lack of pigment on nose.

EARS The ears of the Akita are characteristic of the breed. They are strongly erect and small in relation to rest of head. If ear is folded forward for measuring length, tip will touch upper eye rim. Ears are triangular, slightly rounded at tip, wide at base, set wide on head but not too low, and carried slightly forward over eyes in line with back of neck.
Disqualification: Drop or broken ears.

EYES Dark brown, small, deep-set and triangular in shape. Eye rims black and tight.

LIPS AND TONGUE Lips black and not pendulous; tongue pink.

TEETH Strong with scissors bite preferred, but level bite acceptable. Disqualification: Noticeably undershot or overshot.

NECK AND BODY
NECK Thick and muscular; comparatively short, widening gradually toward shoulders. A pronounced crest blends in with base of skull.

BODY Longer than high, as 10 is to 9 in males, 11 to 9 in bitches. Chest wide and deep; depth of chest is one-half height of dog at shoulder. Ribs well sprung, brisket well developed. Level back with firmly-muscled loin and moderate tuck-up. Skin pliant but not loose.
Serious faults: Light bone, rangy body.

TAIL Large and full, set high and carried over back or against flank in a three-quarter, full or double curl, always dipping to or below level of back. On a three-quarter curl, tip drops well down flank. Root large and strong. Tail bone reaches hock when let down. Hair coarse, straight and full, with no appearance of a plume.
Disqualification: Sickle or uncurled tail.

FOREQUARTERS AND HINDQUARTERS

FOREQUARTERS Shoulders strong and powerful with moderate layback. Forelegs heavy-boned and straight as viewed from front. Angle of pastern 15 degrees forward from vertical. Faults: Elbows in or out, loose shoulders.

HINDQUARTERS Width, muscular development and bone comparable to forequarters. Upper thighs well-developed. Stifle moderately bent and hocks well let down, turning neither in nor out.

DEWCLAWS On front legs generally not removed; dewclaws on hind legs generally removed.

FEET Cat feet, well knuckled up with thick pads. Feet straight ahead.

COAT Double coated. Undercoat thick, soft, dense and shorter than outer coat. Outer coat straight, harsh and standing somewhat off body. Hair on head, legs and ears short. Length of hair at withers and rump approximately two inches, which is slightly longer than on rest of body, except tail, where coat is longest and most profuse.
Faults: Any indication of ruff or feathering.

COLOUR Any colour including white, brindle or pinto. Colours are brilliant and clear and markings are well balanced, with or without mask or blaze. White Akitas have no mask. Pinto has a white background with large, evenly placed patches covering head and more than one-third of body. Undercoat may be a different colour from outer coat.

GAIT Brisk and powerful with strides of moderate length. Back remains strong, firm and level. Rear legs move in line with front legs.

SIZE Males 26 to 28 inches at the withers; bitches 24 to 26 inches. Disqualification: Dogs under 25 inches; bitches under 23 inches.

TEMPERAMENT Alert and responsive, dignified and courageous. Aggressive toward other dogs.

DISQUALIFICATIONS Butterfly nose or total lack of pigmentation on nose. Drop or broken ears. Noticeably undershot or overshot. Sickle or uncurled tail. Dogs under 25 inches; bitches under 23 inches.

Reproduced by kind permission of the American Kennel Club.

Ch. Nor. Ch. Redwitch Dancin' In The Dark: Typifying the British Breed Standard in all departments.

Photo: Keith Allison.

THE BRITISH STANDARD

Although Akitas were shown from the early 1980s in the rare breed and not separately classified sections, it was not until July 30th 1985, after correspondence between the Kennel Club and the proposed breed clubs, that the interim Standard of the Japanese Akita was eventually published. This interim Standard was in force for five years until the breed was awarded Challenge Certificates at Crufts in 1990 and the Official Standard came into force.

THE BRITISH STANDARD

GENERAL APPEARANCE Large, powerful, alert, with much substance and heavy bone.

CHARACTERISTICS Large, broad head, with relatively small eyes and erect ears carried forward in line with back of neck; large, curled tail, in balance with head.

TEMPERAMENT Dignified, courageous, aloof; tends to show dominance over other dogs.

HEAD AND SKULL Large, in balance with body, skull flat, forehead broad, defined stop and clear furrow. Head forms blunt triangle when viewed from above, free from wrinkle. Muzzle broad and strong, cheeks well developed. Nose large and black, bridge straight. Lips tight and black. In white dogs flesh colour pigmentation is permissible on nose and lips. Length from nose to stop is to length from stop to occiput as 2 is to 3.

EYES Relatively small, almond-shaped, clean, moderately set apart and dark brown. Eye rims dark and tight.

EARS Relatively small, thick, triangular, not low set, carried forward over eyes in line with back of neck, firmly erect. Moderately set apart; slightly rounded at tips.

MOUTH Jaws strong, with a perfect, regular and complete scissor bite, i.e. upper teeth closely overlapping lower teeth and set square to the jaws.

NECK Thick and muscular, comparatively short, widening gradually toward shoulders. Pronounced crest blends with back of skull.

FOREQUARTERS Shoulders strong and powerful, moderately laid back. Elbows very tight. Forelegs well boned and straight when viewed from front. Pasterns inclining at approximately 15 degrees.

BODY Longer than high, as 10 is to 9 in males, 11 to 9 in bitches. Chest wide and deep, depth of brisket is one-half height of dog at shoulder. Well-developed forechest. Level back, firmly muscled loin, moderate tuck-up. Skin pliant but not loose.

HINDQUARTERS Strong and muscular, well-developed thighs, moderate turn of stifle. Strong hocks, with only moderate angulation, well let down, turning neither in nor out.

FEET Thick, well-knuckled, very tight, turning neither in nor out. Pads hard. Nails hard. Dewclaws on hind legs customarily removed.

TAIL Large and full, set high, carried over back, full or double curl, always dipping to or below level of back. On a three-quarter curl tail, tip dips down flank. Root large and strong. Hair coarse, straight and full with no appearance of a plume. Sickle or uncurled tail highly undesirable.

GAIT/MOVEMENT Resilient and vigorous with strides of moderate length. Back remains firm and level. Hindlegs move in line with front legs; whilst gaiting will single-track.

COAT Outer coat coarse, straight, and standing off body. Undercoat soft and dense. Coat at withers and rump is approximately 5 cms (2 ins), slightly longer than on rest of body more profuse on tail. No indication of ruff or feathering.

COLOUR Any colour including white brindle or pinto. Colours are

POINTS OF CONFORMATION

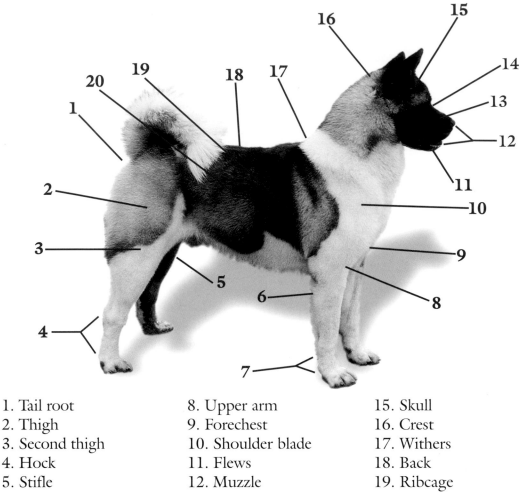

1. Tail root	8. Upper arm	15. Skull
2. Thigh	9. Forechest	16. Crest
3. Second thigh	10. Shoulder blade	17. Withers
4. Hock	11. Flews	18. Back
5. Stifle	12. Muzzle	19. Ribcage
6. Elbow	13. Foreface	20. Loin
7. Pastern	14. Stop	

brilliant and clear. Markings are well defined with or without mask or blaze.

SIZE Height at withers: dogs: 66-71 cms (26-28 ins); bitches: 61-66 cms (24-26 ins).

FAULTS Any departure from the foregoing points should be considered a fault and the seriousness with which the fault should be regarded should be in exact proportion to its degree.

NOTE Male animals should have two apparently normal testicles fully descended into the scrotum.

Reproduced by kind permission of the Kennel Club.

SKELETAL STRUCTURE

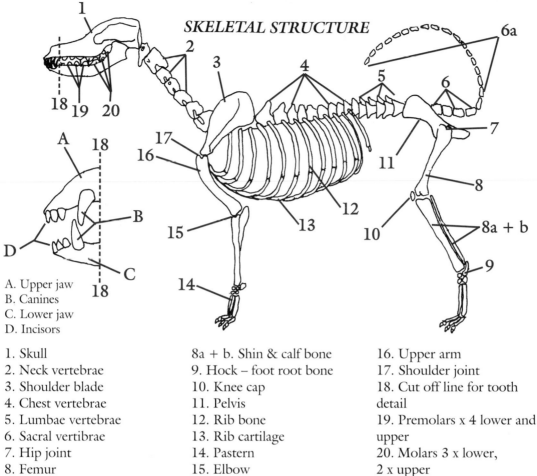

A. Upper jaw
B. Canines
C. Lower jaw
D. Incisors

1. Skull
2. Neck vertebrae
3. Shoulder blade
4. Chest vertebrae
5. Lumbae vertebrae
6. Sacral vertibrae
7. Hip joint
8. Femur

8a + b. Shin & calf bone
9. Hock – foot root bone
10. Knee cap
11. Pelvis
12. Rib bone
13. Rib cartilage
14. Pastern
15. Elbow

16. Upper arm
17. Shoulder joint
18. Cut off line for tooth detail
19. Premolars x 4 lower and upper
20. Molars 3 x lower, 2 x upper

UNDERSTANDING ANGLES

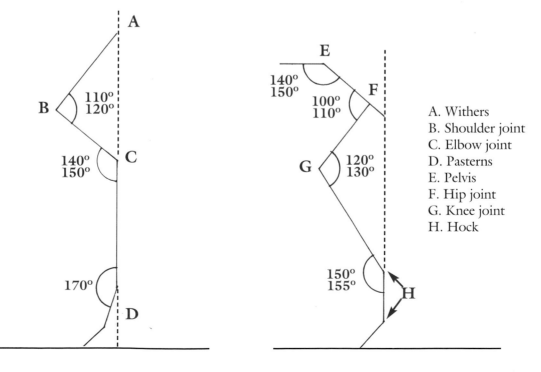

A. Withers
B. Shoulder joint
C. Elbow joint
D. Pasterns
E. Pelvis
F. Hip joint
G. Knee joint
H. Hock

DISCUSSION OF THE STANDARDS

You will now have read the official Standards of the Akita, which set down the facts and help to create the image in your mind. Some people learn facts more easily than others, so to help make that fuzzy picture appear sharp, and turn that basic outline into a proud and dignified Akita, we will expand on each point in the hope that it will help you to understand more about what makes this incredible breed tick.

GENERAL APPEARANCE

While accepting that the Akita is by no means a giant breed, make no mistake, this is still a large dog and as they stand at the moment, the second largest breed in the Utility Group. This is 110lb of pure power, with the bone and substance to match, in fact the complete athlete, with a speed and mobility capable of turning round on a penny. Temperament is best described in the Akita's movement – purposeful with a no-nonsense approach to life, remaining dignified throughout. Character, without doubt, is reserved, silent and dominant and, while the breed does not go looking for trouble, any serious challenge would be met with instant retaliation. To make a comparison, this has to be a thoroughbred stallion in miniature.

HEAD AND SKULL

Over the years, a phrase which has been used to describe a top-quality Akita head, by many doyens of the breed is "superb bear head". So with this in mind, what should we have? A large, blunt triangle, and within that, many more smaller triangles. This large head should be in complete balance to the body, clean and 'dry' with no hint of wrinkle and with well-developed cheeks. A broad strong, muzzle, never narrow or snipy, with tight lips, free from dewlap. Viewed from the side, the head should have a well-defined stop, never so slight as to appear ski-sloped, which will give a weak appearance, nor so abrupt that it becomes Chow-like.

EYES

Although the eyes are one of the parts of the head referred to as triangular, the eyes themselves are, of course, almond-shaped, with the triangle effect being created by colour patterns and eyelids. A relatively small eye, dark in colour and quite deep-set for its own protection – this is one of the main features helping to produce the oriental look, characteristic of many of the Spitz breeds.

EARS

So very important to this breed, yet another triangle on a triangle. Carried strongly erect and small in relation to the head, slightly rounded at the tip and wide at the base. The ear should be thick and well-coated, never thin and German Shepherd-like causing it to tear easily. Viewed from the side, the ear

Northlands Out Of The Shadows, owned by Loren and Christina Egland. A striking head study of pure Japanese lines.

A fabulous head study of Am. Ch. Koma Inu Bronze Bruin, owned and bred by Judythe Dunn.

A super head study showing correct ear-set and placement, correct head proportions and excellent pigmentation.

Photo: Keith Allison

A young bitch showing excellent ear shape with rounded tips. Note the thickness.

Photo: Keith Allison.

A male puppy displaying superb crest of neck, ear carriage and coat quality.

should continue in line with the crest of the neck, tilting slightly forward, and never upright in carriage. Remember, this breed was developed for hunting: the tighter the package, the less chance of damage from an adversary.

MOUTH

Without doubt, this is a powerful jaw, with large canines capable of hanging on to prey. The Standard asks for a complete scissor bite. An unusual feature and one not often commented on, is the relatively small size of the six teeth between the canines. Neither an undershot nor overshot mouth should be accepted, as this would hinder the chances of a hunting dog.

NECK

Although there are relatively few words describing the neck in the Standard, it plays a very important part in the Akita's function – thick and muscular to enable the dog to hold its prey, but short enough to make the Akita less vulnerable to a would-be attacker. The neck should never appear so short that it appears stumpy, nor should it be so long as to appear swan-like, even though the latter is sometimes mistakenly described as elegant. It should appear comparatively short with a pronounced crest blending in with the back of the skull.

FOREQUARTERS

The description in the Breed Standard reads "shoulders strong and powerful". With what we have already described, there is no way they could be anything else! It also says "moderately laid back", which means the shoulder blade will slope at an angle of approximately 50 degrees. The upper arm angles back from the point of shoulder and is the same length. This sets the legs well under the dog, creating the correct construction and producing correct movement. A coiled spring needs added shock-absorbers; any departure from the foregoing would result in the forequarters not functioning properly, causing incorrect movement and ultimately resulting in shoulder damage. These shock absorbers are the pasterns which should slightly incline forward sloping 15° from vertical.

A correct, straight front with tight shoulders and a broad chest.   Photo: Keith Allison.

63

Am. Ch. O'BJ Kings Ransom, owned by Lew and Julie Hoehn. A multi BIS and Group winning dog as well as being a top producer. He typifies the size and substance demanded by the AKC Standard.   *Photo: Booth.*

Tochimuso Of Kurume Hirose: Imported from Japan by Loren and Christina Egland.

BODY

We are now describing the trunk, the centrepiece joining the front to the rear. To maintain balance, it is important that the depth of body is correct. The length of leg to the elbow should be the same as that to the top of the withers. The chest should be broad with well-sprung ribs, giving plenty of heart room and a moderate tuck-up. The back should be straight and firm at all times, even on the move. Narrow fronts and rangy, slab-sided bodies are unacceptable.

Another example of a superb Akita male, showing size, substance and colour, with true head and expression. Am. Ch. Orions Walk The Dinosaur, owned by Debbie DeFonzo.

HINDQUARTERS

No matter how good the front assembly, without the correct rear the movement will still be wrong. We are looking for strong muscular hindquarters, well-developed thighs, a moderate bend of stifle with well let-down hocks. The rear should be broad, never narrow or cow-hocked. A predominant fault seen increasingly in the show ring is total lack of bend of stifle, causing the hock joint to 'pop' right through. This not only happens when the dog is moving but it can occur when the dog is standing still. This is off-putting to the eye; it can cause lameness. The Akita should not be as angulated as the German Shepherd nor as straight behind as the Chow Chow.

Incorrect: A weak cow-hocked rear.
Photo: Keith Allison.

A correct, broad rear with short, strong hocks. Note the excellent tail carriage.
Photo: Keith Allison.

FEET

Although the Standards describe feet well enough, the easiest way to remember them is 'cat-like'. These feet were made for speed and agility, for hanging onto the ground and giving the dog a dexterity which belies the overall size. They should face straight ahead, be well-knuckled and tight, never flat or splayed, which would be a sign of weakness. Dewclaws are normally seen on the front but should be removed from the rear.

TAIL

So important is the correct tail on an Akita that without it, neither the balance nor the complete picture can be fully appreciated. The tail should always be set high and carried over the back in a three-quarter, full or double curl. In the case of a full or double curl, the tail should be coiled on the back; a three-quarter tail should dip down the side of the flank. In no circumstances should it be loose, sickle or gay, or held off the back, as this would denote a low-set or short tail or, more importantly, a questionable temperament. Although in certain circumstances you might see an Akita when totally relaxed, or in extreme heat, holding its tail down, when the dog begins to gait the tail should return immediately to its natural position. The two parts of the tail coat are equally important, not only the coarse, straight hair which can be up to three inches in length, but also the dense undercoat which helps to create the fullness, thus eliminating the effect of a plume which is totally incorrect.

This eager, young bitch shows lovely conformation and shape, with excellent crest and thickness of neck, correct angulation and well-set and well-carried tail.

Northlands Embers At Dawn displays beautiful breed type, an excellent head, good rear angulation, and a well-set tail.

GAIT/MOVEMENT

As in many parts of the Akita Standard, the word 'moderate' appears again, and this is a crucial word in describing movement. This breed should not have the reach and drive seen in the German Shepherd Dog, nor should it be so short-stepping as to appear terrier-like, but the moderate gait should always be brisk and powerful. This is a hunting dog and stamina and endurance play a big part in its intended function. While on the move, the back should at all times remain firm, the back legs moving in line with the front legs. For an Akita to achieve that natural gait he must be sound in body and mind.

COAT

It is very important that time be taken to understand the Akita's coat. In many circumstances a short plush coat, which can appear very attractive has been mistaken for the correct type. The Akita should carry a superb double coat. The undercoat is short, soft and dense, almost wool-like. The outer coat is straight and harsh and stands off the body, protecting the dog from extreme cold and also providing a water-proof jacket. The guard-hair is hard and glossy and stands out through the underlying double coat.

Variation in length is very important, the overall body coat length being

MOVEMENT
Photos: Keith Allison.

A young male with excellent front and rear movement. The side gait shows effortless movement, with correct reach and drive, while retaining a totally firm topline.

approximately three-quarters of an inch, with the guard-hair standing through it. As the crest of the neck flows into the withers, the length increases to approximately two inches, as does that on the rump. The coat is at its longest on the tail where it can reach up to three inches. There should, however, be no sign of ruff or feathering. As with the German Shepherd, long-coated Akitas can be produced from certain breedings, and although these make super pets, this is a fault and the long-coats should not be shown or bred from.

COLOUR
The Standard allows for all colours, but describes them as "brilliant and clear". The undercoat is often a different colour from the outer coat and the guard hair can be different again. So let us define 'clear' This means, on a white dog, or where there are white markings, that there should be no sign of 'ticking' or freckles showing through the white coat. The Standard says "brilliant": this does not mean that all Akitas have to be red and white or black and white. Fawns can be brilliant and clear as long as they are a true, rich colour and not a pale, washed out or muddy fawn.

Pinto is defined as a white background with large, evenly placed patches covering the head and more than one third of the body. All mask colours are equally acceptable, whether they be black, white, self-coloured (the same colour as the body), or a split mask.

Although all colours are equally acceptable, the markings can sometimes be displeasing to the eye, and while we do not recognise the term 'mismark', the markings should not detract either from the expression or from the dignity of the Akita.

SIZE
The Standard's requirement is Dogs 26ins to 28ins (66cm to 71cm) and Bitches 24ins to 26ins (61cm to 66cm). This allows a difference of two inches and for a breeder this should be

A top-quality head showing a very evenly marked split mask.

Photo: Hartley.

enough. With this in mind a 25ins male is as incorrect as a 29ins male. Bigger is not better, although soundness in the former may be easier to achieve. Again, the word 'moderate' springs to mind, and over the years it is interesting to note that most top winners have fitted into the 26ins to 27ins bracket.

FAULTS

There are no disqualifying faults in the British Standard, and neither should there be 'fault judging'. Every dog has good and bad points, and while the seriousness of each fault must be taken into account, it is the overall type and soundness of the animal that matters.

DIFFERENTIATING BETWEEN THE STANDARDS

Although basically very similar, there are still some points which differ in the British and American Standards.

While discussing the head, the American Standard says "free of wrinkle when at ease", thereby suggesting wrinkle is acceptable when the dog is alert. The British Standard says "free from wrinkle"– in other words, at all times.

Under Teeth, the American Standard asks for a scissor bite but will accept a level one, whereas the British Standard calls for a scissor bite only. Probably because of this, it has taken some considerable time to eliminate the level bite from the Akita in Britain, and even now it will still re-appear in a breeding

programme from time to time.

Probably the most controversial difference is the word used to describe the temperament. While the British Standard calls for "dominance" over dogs, the American Standard spells it out as "aggressive". This one word leaves the would-be purchaser in no doubt about the Akita's feelings towards other dogs. While aggressiveness towards people is totally unacceptable, we should also accept that this is a dominant breed who will stand no nonsense with other canines.

While the British Standard has no disqualifying faults, the American lists five. We find it interesting that the first four of these make no allowances for any detraction from the Standard; in other words, the fault is a disqualifying fault. However, the fifth relates to the height, which has a minimum, but it also permits a further one inch between the disqualifying fault and the Standard to be accepted. At times this can be confusing.

There is, we are sure, no argument about the fact that since the war, the Akita in Japan has changed tremendously. Interestingly, though, in the first part of the FCI Standard under General Appearance, a "large-sized dog, sturdily built with much substance" is still called for, thus agreeing with both American and British Standards. However, when comparing the two, the Japanese type is often a lighter-framed and less sturdy animal.

Under temperament, while the American states "aggressive" and the British "dominant" towards other dogs, we find under the same heading in the FCI Standard the words "faithful, docile and receptive". The word docile must be very misleading when considering the fact that in the show ring in Japan, Akitas are exhibited sparring terrier-like against each other. Would an aggressive or dominant dog or a docile dog do this?

Another confusing point is made under the 'Head' section. Although the wording in all the Standards is basically the same, the FCI asks for the muzzle to be broad at the base, strong and moderately long, tapering but not pointed. This is more consistent with the modern Japanese head.

Colour is obviously where the Standards differ tremendously, with only four colours, all with reverse mask, being accepted by the FCI. It is beyond dispute that before the war, the earlier Standards accepted all colours including black masks.

Only three disqualifying faults are listed in the FCI Standard, but there are nine under the heading of faults which should be judged according to the degree of seriousness. One of these nine is the black mask, which as we have already pointed out, was heavily penalised, not as a fault but as a disqualifying fault.

6 SHOWING THE AKITA

Having carefully selected your prospective future Champion you should begin to prepare the dog for the show ring months ahead of your first event. There are many reasons for this. Of paramount importance is the need to get your dog fit, with good muscle tone. This is no different than training an athlete. The Akita needs a regular work-out routine. Your way of life, and the facilities you have around you, will determine how you can go about this. Not all of us are lucky enough to live in the countryside with access to land around us, but living in a town house should not mean that your dog does not get the correct exercise.

PREPARATION
Road walking at a brisk pace a couple of times a day is an excellent way of building a dog up. You should also find a park or open ground where you can put your Akita on a flexi-lead, so he can run and really stretch those limbs out.

Running free: Without doubt, the best way of stretching those limbs is to allow an Akita free exercise in a controlled environment.   *Photo: Keith Allison.*

71

Running alongside a bike is good for both you and your dog, as long as you have firm control and, with today's modern equipment, even if you do not have a large garden, a jogging machine fits quite easily into a garage. It is surprising how many people use these to exercise their dogs these days, when time and facilities are at a premium. But for those of us who are lucky enough to have purpose-built paddocks, there is no substitute for free-running, where exercising two dogs, side by side, will stretch those muscles better than can be achieved in any other way.

The dog's weight should be checked daily, as weight-gain cannot be rectified overnight. Excessive weight alters both the top line and attitude; an extra few pounds can make the difference between a dog striding out or hanging back on the lead. Neither is being too lean correct, as the Breed Standard calls for substance but not fat. So you are really playing a balancing act to ensure your dog hits the ring in the peak of condition. Many things can affect weight, apart from overeating. We have seen a stud dog drop pounds in days when there are bitches in season around him, and the bitches can also lose weight at this time.

Something we tend to forget is that, in a busy show season, hundreds of miles are travelled each week, with the dogs sleeping in crates. We know how this affects us and it can have the same stressful effect on the dogs. We find it

helpful to carry as much of our own water as we can, as the change of water in different areas can also affect them.

If this is beginning to sound like 'hard work', then the answer is 'it is' – but the more you put into it, the more your dog will respond.

GROOMING
As a newcomer, grooming is not something you can learn overnight, neither is it merely putting a brush through the dog's coat the night before the show. Presentation is tremendously important in a show dog and there is no substitute for experience, nor is there any substitute for a hands-on demonstration. However, over the next few paragraphs, we will attempt to take you through a step-by-step procedure and, hopefully, finish with your Akita bathed and groomed and ready for the show ring.

BATHING
You are about to discover just how much insulation your Akita's coat carries. It is there not just to keep the dog warm, but to be completely waterproof. To get right through that dense undercoat is a job and a half. In an ideal world you need a bath with shower facilities over it but, obviously, some people have to resort to a hosepipe, or even copious buckets of water.

Now you have the dog in the bath you need to soak him right through,

BATHING AND DRYING

Photos: Keith Allison.

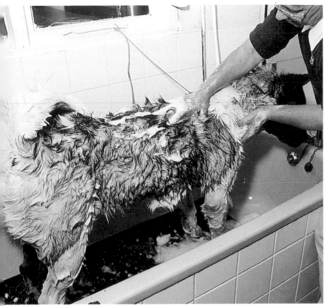

An Akita male being bathed. For security reasons he is tied, and he is standing on a non-slip mat.

A high-powered dryer is the fastest way of removing moisture from the coat.

There are times when standing too close to your dog does not pay off!

Use a cool hair-dryer for the finishing touches.

and we do mean right through. Having already selected your shampoo, it is easier to have this pre-mixed and ready in a jug. There are several ideal dog shampoos on the market, and these are far better than using household detergents or washing-up liquid, which will have a harmful effect on the coat and remove the natural oils. If your Akita has any badly stained areas, we suggest rubbing full-strength shampoo into these first so that they can be soaking while you bath the rest of your dog.

Now apply the shampoo to the rest of the dog, working it thoroughly into the coat. All areas need to be bathed, including the ears and under the belly, where the coat can be particularly grimy from the dog lying down. Pay extra attention to the tail, particularly if it is white, as it can really help to set an Akita off. Nothing looks worse than yellow staining on areas that should be bright white. When you are sure you have not missed anywhere, you can start rinsing. This should be repeated until you have removed all traces of soap from the coat, not only because traces of soap could be harmful to the skin, but also because it hinders the drying process.

Once rinsed, squeeze as much water from the coat as possible by pushing firmly with the hands down the back, across the chest and down the legs. Now, as quickly as possible, get your Akita to an area where he can shake, as he or she will do this vigorously, especially at the wrong time, leaving you wondering who was having the bath, you or your dog!

DRYING

The next step is up on to the grooming table, which by now your dog should be thoroughly used to. We find the aid of a 'blaster', or high-powered dryer, invaluable at this time, as it not only propels the water from the coat but removes dead and loose hair as well.

When your Akita is seventy-five per cent dry, switch to a normal hand-held hair dryer and use this in combination with your rake. Take care not to use the dryer too hot or too close, or you will burn or damage the coat. As you dry, lift the coat with the rake away from the body to give a stand-off effect. This applies to all parts of the dog, apart from the point of withers, and along the back to the base of the tail. Pay particular attention to the head and cheeks; even the ears should be combed through.

This is a very time-consuming process and, when completed, you should be able to put your rake through the coat in all four directions – up, down, and from side to side.

If you cannot do this then your Akita has not been properly groomed. However, your dog now should be completely transformed and look a picture, so let us get down to the finer details.

NAILS

Where your Akita lives, and the surfaces the dog normally runs on, will determine whether the nails are naturally kept short or if they need a helping hand. Remember, the Standard asks for cat-like feet and you never see nails showing on a cat. If circumstances allow your dog's nails to grow then you will need to trim them back. This can be done through the use of a set of nail clippers in conjunction with a small wood file or, better still, a battery-operated nail grinder. The other thing you should also check for is the amount of hair growing between the pads on the foot. If this is excessive, it should be trimmed back level with the pad.

NAIL-CLIPPING AND FEET TRIMMING
Photos: Keith Allison.

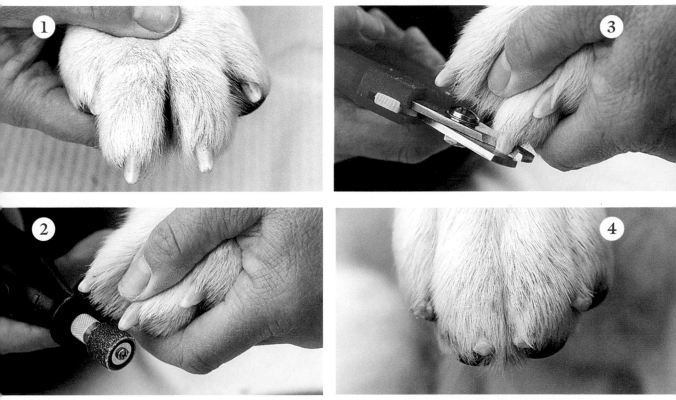

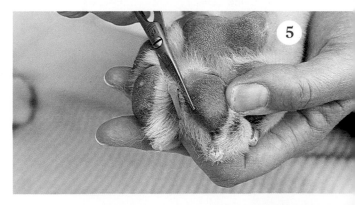

1. Nails in need of clipping.

2. Using a nail grinder.

3. Take extra care when using nail clippers.

4. The round, cat-like appearance called for in the Standard.

5. Trim the excess hair that grows between the pads.

TEETH

This aspect of grooming is so very important, as teeth are something that every single judge looks at, and so many exhibitors fail to bother with. Dirty teeth leave a lasting impression on many judges, so you should ensure that any tartar build-up is removed, not only from the canines but from the molars as well. This can be done with the aid of a tooth de-scaler but, if you do not possess one, then a coin will help chip the tartar away equally well. Not only will the teeth look better after this treatment, but your dog will feel a whole lot better too.

TEETH CLEANING
Photos: Keith Allison.

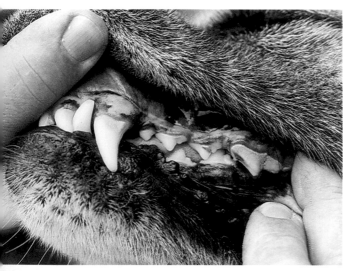

Dirty teeth showing an accumulation of tartar.

A coin is equally effective for chipping off the tartar.

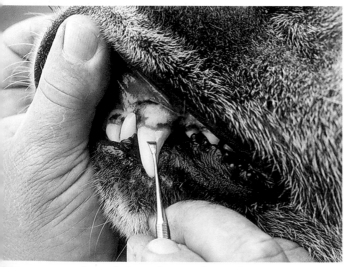

A tooth de-scaler can be used.

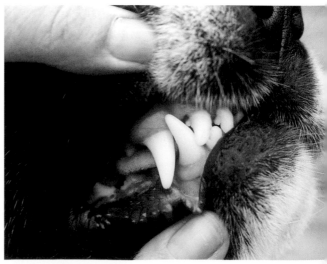

The end result – white, healthy teeth.

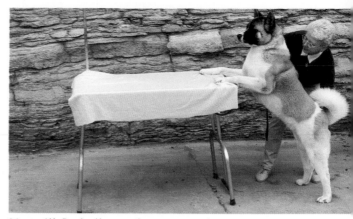

You will find all procedures are easier to carry out if your Akita has learnt to stand quietly and calmly on a grooming table.
Step One: Place the front legs on the table.

EARS

Although, as a breed, the Akita is not prone to ear problems, ears should also be checked on a routine basis to ensure they are kept clean and free from mites, particularly if you have cats around.

COAT CARE

Nowhere on your Akita's coat should scissoring ever be necessary, apart from under the pads and where there is a personal preference about removing the whiskers from the muzzle and eyebrows. Some people prefer the clean outline which removing them leaves, while others prefer the natural look.

The Akita's coat tends to blow twice a year, with the spring change generally being heavier than the autumn one. The first signs of blowing are usually little tufts sticking out of the legs and, as the coat loosens, these then appear up the flanks, chest and shoulders with the body coat being the last to blow. This can take up to three weeks and the best way of dealing with it is to remove the dead and loose hair as often as possible. We do not, however, recommend raking while the coat is dry, as this can break or damage it; so, even if you do not want to bath your dog every time you strip the coat out, you should at least spray with water to dampen the coat down, then blow with a hair dryer while raking out to remove dead hair.

Once your dog is back in full coat, very little grooming is necessary, apart from preparing for a show. However,

Step Two: Gently lift the rear.

Step Three: Fasten the head-collar so that your Akita is safe and secure while being groomed.

ROUTINE COAT CARE
Photos: Keith Allison.

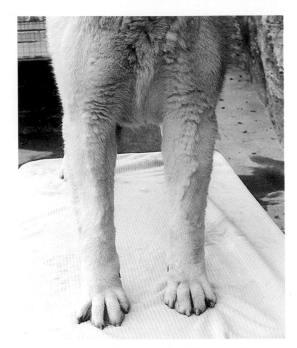

An ungroomed dog bitch in full coat-blow.

After: The leg has now been groomed thoroughly. Note the amount of hair loss.

Males should be checked regularly for sore patches on the testicles.

Before: Hair is hanging from the rear leg.

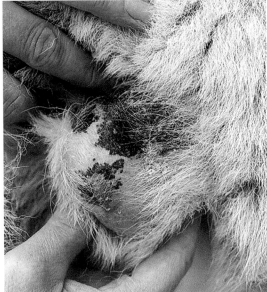

SHOW PRESENTATION
Photos: Keith Allison.

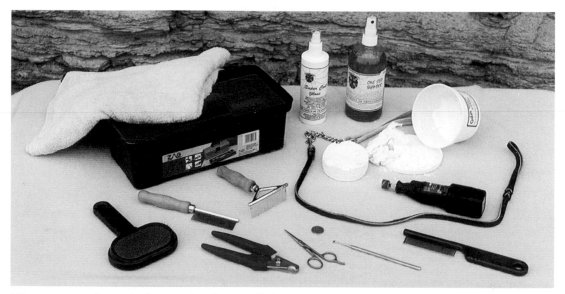

The contents of a typical grooming box – all the items are necessary in order to keep your Akita in tip-top condition.

GROOMING YOU AKITA
Photo: Michael Trafford.

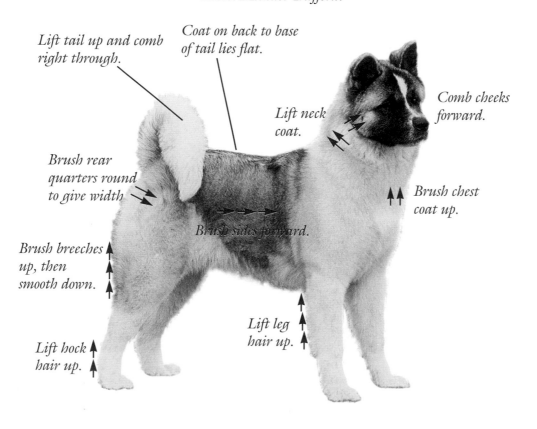

Lift tail up and comb right through.

Coat on back to base of tail lies flat.

Comb cheeks forward.

Lift neck coat.

Brush rear quarters round to give width

Brush chest coat up.

Brush sides forward.

Brush breeches up, then smooth down.

Lift leg hair up.

Lift hock hair up.

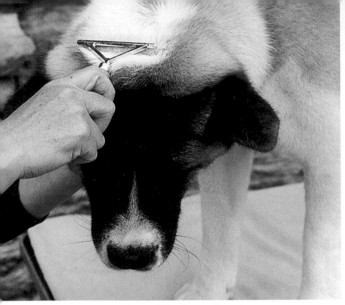

Use a rake to lift the neck hair.

Use a comb to encourage the cheeks forwards.

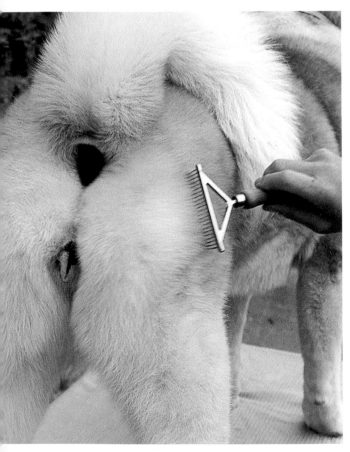

The rake is used throughout the coat. Here, the hindquarters are being finished.

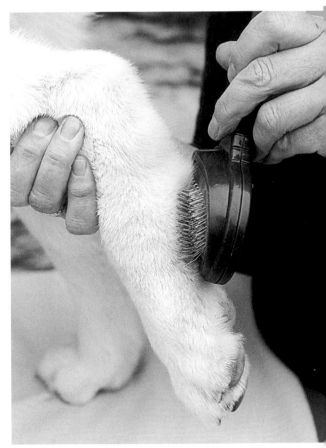

The pin-brush is used to lift the hair on the hock.

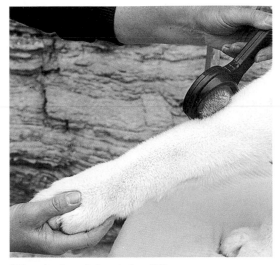

The pin-brush is used to lift the hair on the front leg.

Hold the tip of the tail and comb downwards.

you should routinely check nails, teeth and coat for any problems, particularly through the summer when ticks and fleas are about. A bath in a good insecticidal shampoo will do no harm at this time. Some Akitas are also prone to pressure sores on elbows and hocks and we find antibiotic creams and a topical lubricant help with these. Where males are concerned, regular checking of the testicles is essential, as they are prone to rubbing them while sitting or lying on concrete or certain carpets, causing irritation or sores. If this is not treated with an antibiotic cream, it will result in an increase in temperature in the scrotum, and so affect the quality of the sperm produced. If left untreated for a long period of time, it could easily lead to the male going sterile.

RING TRAINING
Having spent the first few months of your puppy's life socialising and lead-training, ring-training can commence at around four months. Do it any earlier and we find that the puppy can become bored very quickly with the whole procedure.

Practise standing your pup on a grooming table and lifting the legs and feet, so the dog becomes accustomed to having them placed in the correct position. Gently lift the lips and look at the teeth using the command 'teeth', so that puppy learns that having the mouth examined is routine. This should only take up about five minutes per day at

Top American professional handler Ed Finnegan Jnr teaching a puppy to stand on a grooming table.

The puppy must learn to stand four-square on the ground.   *Photo: Hartley.*

this age and, once the pup is happy with it, transfer to training on the floor.

Repeat the table procedure until the puppy is relaxed and will stand for a few minutes without any fuss, then practise trotting up and down with puppy on a loose lead. Of tremendous benefit at this time are local training clubs, where you can seek the help and advice of more experienced handlers and trainers. These clubs also help with socialising and introduce you to competition through the matches which are arranged.

HANDLING AND PRESENTATION

Hopefully, you will now have been bitten by the showing bug, so, assuming that your puppy is ready for it, you can progress to the local open shows or matches and then, with a little luck, to Championship shows. You already know the basics of handling your puppy, but you now need to learn how to present your dog to the best advantage for the judge.

First of all, allow yourself plenty of time when arriving at a show, so you are not panicking to get into the ring, as this will immediately transfer down the lead and unsettle your puppy. Check the numbers in your class and try to aim for the middle of the line, so you can watch what the judge requires of the other exhibitors before you have to do it yourself. If the venue is outdoors, carefully examine the ground where you will be standing your dog to ensure that

Training a young male to free-stand and bait by watching for the tidbit in your pocket.

STACKING
Photos: Keith Allison.

Place the front legs.

Adjust the rear legs.

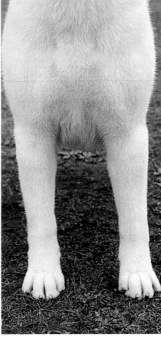

A correctly stacked front.

A correctly stacked rear.

The end result.

it is level. Front feet standing in a hole can make a vast difference to what should be a level topline, so always aim to pose your dog on a flat surface.

When it is your turn to set up for the judge, walk the dog into place by holding the lead in your left hand and supporting the chin in your right, using it as a brake. If a dog is built correctly, it will stand correctly and, basically, should come to a stop in a four-square position. However, slight adjustments may have to be made, so, if the front is not quite parallel, ease the dog over by pushing gently on the chin, which will probably bring the legs into line. If further adjustment is still required, decide which leg is in the more correct position and move the other leg to match it. Do this by holding the collar in the right hand, if moving the left leg, or vice versa, and grasping the leg firmly by the elbow and lowering it into position parallel with the other one. Never stand the legs wider than the dog's chest, as this will give an unbalanced appearance.

Having set the front up, you now need to adjust the rear. This should never be done by just snatching at the leg, but by running the hand from the neck, all the way down the body and the flank, and then picking the hock up and placing it in position. This will give your dog confidence, as he will know where you are coming from and what you are doing.

Now your Akita is stacked up, you need to check the tail, to ensure it is correctly set on the back, and you need to attract the dog's attention to give the true expression and ear carriage to complete the picture. We are often asked about the use of bait and there is no doubt that this can be useful to make your dog alert. However, a puppy should be excited and bouncy and interested in its surroundings, so full advantage should be taken of this, with a good handler letting the pup focus on either the judge or the ringside attractions. Although there will be days when everything does not quite go to plan, as long as the basic training is there your Akita should improve at each attempt.

While the judge is carrying out his examination, talk to your dog to give reassurance that all is well. A nervous handler can bring out the guarding instinct in an Akita.

MOVING YOUR AKITA
You must realise that the lead is an extension of your arm and, just as a writer uses a pen, so a handler uses the lead. Your dog should be encouraged to move out with style. Nothing looks worse than an unwilling Akita being dragged around the ring. You will be asked to run straight across and back, in a triangle or in a full circle. For the straight across and back, you should fix your eye on something directly across the ring. Hold the lead fairly taut, about a yard from the dog's head, take a circle

David in the Group ring at Crufts 1984 with Ch. Goshens Bigger Is Better At Redwitch. He is in total harmony with the dog, showing complete control with style and ease.
Photo: Dalton.

in front of the judge to walk the dog into the correct pace, and take a direct line, not deviating from one side or the other. This will produce a smooth rear action, allowing the judge to assess the dog's rear movement correctly.

When doing a triangle or full circle, you want to produce a free-flowing movement. Ensure you have the collar and lead in the correct place, with the collar right up under the chin and the clasp at the side of the right ear, and

encourage your Akita to run out a yard in front of you. It is very important to find the correct pace that suits both you and your dog and, to create the right picture, you need to be in harmony together, neither letting the other down.

On completion of your movement, you need to bring your dog into a stand position in front of the judge. As this is one of the last impressions he/she will have, it should be neat and tidy and not so near that the judge has to step back, nor so far away that the dog's head and expression cannot be seen.

You should then return to the line-up and prepare to stack your dog, ready for the judge's final assessment. Do not crowd the handler in front of you or block out the one behind. Pay attention to the judge at all times and listen to his commands carefully. If the class is asked to gait round the ring together, leave yourself plenty of room from the dog in front so that your movement is not restricted; puppies may be over-playful running round, adult males will certainly not.

There are few natural handlers; it is not everybody's forte in life and some people find it extremely hard, but the more you work at it and practise, the better you will become. No two dogs handle alike and adjustments have to be made to suit each one; only experience will help you understand the techniques involved. Without doubt, the best way of learning is to watch the top handlers and, if possible, video them at work, so you can sit at home and study their technique at your leisure.

7 *JUDGING THE AKITA*

One of the greatest honours in the dog world is being asked to judge one's breed at Championship or Breed Club level. However, acceptance of this appointment should not be given lightly, as it is, indeed, a great responsibility. Before undertaking this task, years should have been spent gaining a thorough knowledge of the breed, attending seminars, watching top judges and breed specialists judging the Akita and making sure that you know, and understand, the Breed Standard from beginning to end.

One excellent way of helping to gain this experience is to steward as much as possible, especially for top judges where knowledge of ring procedure and etiquette can be invaluable. Never be afraid to ask, as most senior officials are only too happy to help and share their knowledge. Remember that while you are judging the dogs, you are being judged. Far too many people rush into

judging before they are ready. This is a big mistake; you should only take on a judging appointment when you are sure you have enough experience and also have the respect of fellow exhibitors and breeders.

PRACTICALITIES
Having taken the big step and accepted a judging appointment, there are certain things to bear in mind to ensure that the day goes smoothly. Punctuality is crucial, both for your own peace of mind and for that of the club secretary, who needs to know that you are on site and ready to begin on time. If the appointment is several hours away, then travel the night before in order to avoid those early morning traffic queues on the nation's highways; and also remember to avoid the jams which can occur just getting into the show ground. It also helps to have ten minutes by yourself, after you arrive, with a cup of coffee, to calm your

nerves, especially with your first appointment – and then report to the secretary in plenty of time to collect your judge's folder. It is important at this time to sit down and study the breakdown of the class numbers. In a large entry at Championship show level, some classes may have between twenty and thirty Akitas entered. Ring size needs to be taken into account and start and finish times gauged so you do not end up having to rush the last few classes to ensure that the Best of Breed winner is selected before the Group is called.

Allow yourself ten minutes before the start of judging to introduce yourself to your ring stewards – experienced ones are worth their weight in gold. Check where the judging table is and agree with the stewards how you want your ring set out. Remember, it is just as important for the exhibitors to have a good view as it is for yourself. Decide where you want your final line-up to be, and also where you want seen dogs from previous classes to stand, as confusion does not build confidence.

Make sure your judge's book is correctly and clearly filled in and signed. This is something you should do yourself and not allow your steward to do for you. As there is little room in the book for critiques, you should have with you either a notepad or a Dictaphone – whichever you feel most comfortable with. A written critique is a very important part of your judging

duties in the UK and should be forwarded to the dog press as soon as possible. In America no critique is expected, but in some European countries you are required to give an immediate one on every single dog.

One last point: make sure you are suitably attired for your appointment. Smart but sensible are the key words. Remember, the dogs are on show, not you. Loose scarves, floppy hats and floaty skirts are all things which can distract or even unnerve some dogs. Sensible, comfortable shoes are a must and, even on the best of days, a complete wet-weather outfit is worth having in the car – especially for the unpredictable seasons.

RING MANNERS

The main thing to remember, having accepted an appointment to judge the breed, is that every single exhibitor, whether their dog is good, bad or indifferent, is entitled to the same amount of your time, attention and courtesy.

When you have decided where you want your dogs to be placed while you go over them, stand everyone in that same spot. The same applies to moving the dog. If you have decided on a triangle and then straight across and back, make sure you repeat this with every exhibit.

With large entries, use your stewards to bring forward the next dog, ready for judging, while you are finishing

Take them round please! Judge Martin Freeman examines the dogs on the move at WELKS 1993.

assessing the movement of the previous one. This saves time and also helps calm the exhibitors, as they do not feel pressured into standing their dog in a rush.

It is very important to keep your concentration on the job in hand and not to be distracted by events in other rings or to engage in conversation at ringside while still judging dogs. This is not only very bad ring manners but can also give exhibitors totally the wrong impression. In large classes, do not be afraid to short-list and re-run the dogs you wish to assess again and, when you have decided on your placements, do it decisively, with confidence. Above all, be honest with your opinions. You are there to judge the dogs, not the people, no matter who has bred them or who owns them. If you cannot honestly give the best dog on the day Best of Breed, no matter who is at the end of the lead, or you can be intimidated inside or outside the ring, you should not be judging in the first place.

Judge Jackie Ransom examines her Open Dog line-up at Crufts 1995.

Judge Ken Bullock examining Ch. Lizda Zee Zee Flash at the City of Birmingham Utility Group.
She went on to take Reserve in the Group. (There were only two Group places at that time.)

Judge June Freeman examines the head of Redwitch Another Legend at Bournemouth 1998.   Photo: Carol Ann Johnson.

APPROACHING THE AKITA

You now have your first Akita stacked up in front of you. Stand back and take a long look. You cannot assess the shape and outline if you are on top of the dog. The overall balance, the set of the ears and the tail carriage are the things which should immediately strike you.

Having assessed the outline, walk round the front of the dog, stand back a yard and take a good look at the head. This is a 'head' breed, and there are many important features to assess here. Remember the Standard and look for those triangles. Look at the ear

placement, size and shape; so many judges forget the importance of the ears. Look for the colour, size and set of the eyes, the stop and the strength of muzzle. Moving down, look for the width and depth of chest, the front assembly, length of leg, pasterns and those cat-like feet. Now think – what you see should be impressive; does it balance?

We are now ready to move forward and examine the dog. We personally have a list of 'do nots' which we have accumulated over the years, by watching the mistakes made by others

Mrs Freeman checks the body and coat. Redwitch Another Legend went on to take the Dog CC and BOB.

Photo: Carol Ann Johnson.

with a lesser understanding of the character and temperament of the Akita.

The breed's natural instinct is to be aloof with strangers. As a judge, you are that stranger. Never make prolonged eye contact, as an Akita, particularly a male, may construe this as a challenge. You should never hold the dog by his cheeks – he will take great exception to this. Excessive pressure over the shoulders and withers while examining the dog may be taken as a dominance threat, and a real quirk of the Akita is taking exception to having his legs and feet picked up. We do not know the reason for this, but over the years we have seen even the soundest of temperaments ruffled by this action.

Over-zealous handling is neither necessary nor advisable.

Now you must decide whether you wish to examine the teeth yourself or whether you wish the handler to show them to you to minimise cross-infection. Whatever you decide, you should follow the same pattern with all the dogs.

Having satisfied yourself as far as the mouth is concerned, you should then move on round the side. Take time to study the crest of the neck and shoulder placement and evaluate the coat length and texture. Check the hindquarters for muscle tone and shape, and take a long look at that tail – the set, the length, the carriage; does it balance the head? One of our own personal pet hates is the

Ch. Claran Blue Velvet By Vormund, stacked up and preparing for the judge's examination.

judge who immediately takes the tail off the back to measure it to the hock. We spend hours preparing babies for the show ring and the first thing that happens to them is that a stranger pushes their tail into an unnatural position. You should be able to evaluate the tail as it is carried naturally, balancing the whole dog. Even a badly set, incorrect tail will still touch the hock so – what is the point of upsetting the dog? Some Akitas carry their tail naturally on the right non-judging side, so be prepared to walk round to assess it as it is, and not try to make it do something which is not comfortable for the dog.

A superb shot of Am. Ch. Tobe's Return Of The Jeddai baiting for handler Sue Capone.

Now stand back and take a look at the rear, the overall conformation, the hocks, and check for two testicles in males. Take a last look at the side picture, then move back to the front and give instruction to the handler where you want them to move.

As a judge, it is essential to understand the importance of colour in the Akita, as it is a very eye-catching, attractive breed. However, our own personal opinion is that breed-type, soundness, construction and movement are what makes an Akita, and, whereas we all have our own personal preferences in colour, surely type and soundness must come first.

Remember that, as judges, none of us are perfect, we all make mistakes, but with practice and dedication, we can all get better.

MERITS *v* FAULTS
There is no doubt that any one can fault-judge, and the perfect Akita has never been bred. How often have you stood at the ringside listening to novices condemning the top dog of the moment for any single fault! Taking into account that the Breed Standard has no disqualifying faults, then it is, without doubt, virtues we must be looking for. All things being equal, final decisions should be made on the merits of a dog, and on where it excels over its rivals, rather than condemning others because they carry the judge's personal pet hate.

STRUCTURE AND MOVEMENT
Although the Akita is found in the Utility Group in the UK, we must not forget that, essentially, this is a working breed, bred originally for hunting, and this must, therefore, be reflected in its movement.

When judging the breed, you should be looking for a dog capable of showing

Crufts 1998: Judge Meg Purnell-Carpenter deciding BOB between Dog CC Ch. Nor. Ch. Redwitch Dancin' In The Dark and Bitch CC Yakitori Yesates.

Ch. Overhills Cherokee Lite-Fut showing typical reach and drive.

An ideal judge's view of correct side gait as Ch. Am. Ch. Tarmalanes Veni Vidi Vici goes through his paces.

power, strength, agility and endurance. If the Akita's construction is right, with the correct ratios, then this should produce strides of moderate length. While watching side gait, the top line should be held firm at all times, with a reasonable forward reach and an effortless rear drive which is not excessive or high-kicking, as this would be wasting energy, something which a hunting dog is not accustomed to doing.

When viewing the movement across and back, the Akita's front action should show good width of chest, with straight firm legs which slightly converge to the centre line. Weak and loose pasterns will give an all-too-common flicking action. The rear action should be of equal width, strong and firm, with no sign of looseness. It is interesting to note that, if you run an Akita on wet sand, you will clearly see that while gaiting, he will single track.

Judging the movement is definitely not the easiest part of assessing the whole dog, as excellent movers are few and far between, and what looks sensational stacked up very often falls apart on the move. However, movement is an essential part of a hunting dog's life, so it must be high on the list of priorities when judging.

8 TIPS FROM THE TOP

It takes a lifetime to build up the knowledge, experience and expertise to breed, rear and handle top-quality purebred dogs. All too often, this great wealth of information is lost as generation succeeds generation, and the world of dogs is the poorer for it.

The Akita is a relatively new breed in the western world, and in an attempt to pool resources, four top breeders have been selected to give their own views and to relate their own experiences in response to a series of questions that were put to them.

CATHERINE BELL, Daijobu Akitas, Knoxville, Tennessee.

Q. When did you first become interested in purebred dogs and what was the first breed you owned and why?

A. My first pedigree dog was a German Shepherd which I owned during the 1970s and which was chosen purely as a companion, as at that time I was not interested in showing or breeding.

Q. When did you first buy an Akita and did you buy it as a show dog, as foundation stock or just as a pet ?

A. The beginning of the most wonderful years in the dog world came in the form of a gift. We had heard very little about the Akita breed and this was our first real interest in pure-bred dogs. The year was 1981 and Maxwell's Kuro Ban Kuma soon became Champion Maxwell's Kuro Ban Kuma. To this day we owe a debt of gratitude to the Maxwells for this great bitch who, from very limited breedings, produced many Champions, thus establishing the Daijobu line.

Q. Who had the biggest influence on you in your first years in the breed and why?

A. We next purchased a male Akita from a well-known breeder, the late Robert

Campbell of the Okii Yubi kennel. We were desperately trying to educate ourselves on the Akita and, as there was little written material available, we had many occasions to communicate with Mr Campbell in person, actually 'picking his brain' with regard to the breed. This proved very valuable in choosing the direction we wanted our breeding programme to follow.

Q. As a very successful breeder yourself, what other Akita breeder do you most admire and why?

A. We soon had the pleasure of meeting another very knowledgeable breeder who set the pace for our kennel. Edward J. Finnegan Jnr. had been showing and breeding Akitas for several years and he came to our rescue, handling our dogs in the show ring and finishing at least fifteen to their Championship and many of those to Group placements. We were lucky enough to have Ed help us with our pedigrees and teach us the important aspects of successful breeding. By using his stud dog, Ch. Yuko's Happy Grizzly ROM at stud, who was a wonderful example of the Akita breed, we combined two great lines that produced type, soundness and extremely even temperaments. We cannot thank Ed enough for the wealth of education and knowledge that he shared and for being a trusting friend. Another name we must mention is that of Fran Wassermann of the Date Tensha kennel. Her knowledge of the breed was tremendous and of great help to us personally. She was always honest in her opinions, always telling it as it was, not just what we wanted to hear, and she paved the way to many successful breedings as Ed had done.

Q. Which is the most successful show dog you have owned or bred and what points do you attribute to his or her success ?

A. The most successful Akita from the Daijobu line was as near to the Standard as any dog or bitch could be. Ch. Daijobu's Nichi-Ko had type, soundness and attitude – so important in a show dog. She won many Best of Breeds over the males, many Group placements and finished Number One Akita Bitch in the US for 1986.

Am. Ch. Daijobu's Nichi-Ko bred and owned by Catherine and Charles Bell.

Q. When breeding, what do you consider to be the most important features of the breed?

A. Sound, healthy Akitas had to be our prime concern. We always X-rayed for possible problems with hip dysplasia, and had eyes examined for Progressive Retinal Atrophy (PRA). Knowing the Standard of your breed is so important, and breeding to adhere to it as near as possible. We checked and rechecked pedigrees and researched several generations behind our choice of sire for possible health problems. We were also careful to breed for good temperament to ensure our Akitas were sound in mind as well as body.

Q. How important do you deem colour to be when picking a show puppy?

A. Colour is probably the last factor considered when we choose a puppy. Sure, a well marked pinto or a beautiful red with flashy, white markings are desirable and make a beautiful picture. But if that attractively marked dog is not healthy, or does not adhere to the Standard, what do you have ? Nothing that will help improve the breed.

Q. How much of your success do you put down to:
a) line breeding
b) in-breeding
c) out-crossing?

A. With the strength of the Standard in our lines we chose to stay with this in our breeding programme. Line breeding was our choice and this helped us decide which sire to choose when breeding a litter. Continual in-breeding will result in the loss of the ideal Standard of the Akita and an out-cross breeding should be done if this happens.

Q. What points do you think contributed to making your kennel so successful and what advice would you give to a newcomer in the breed?

A. Knowing the reason for breeding each litter is so important and planning each one accordingly. Being able to seek and accept advice from breeders more knowledgeable than ourselves helped us tremendously and we spent time researching and learning about the Akita. Also, having excellent lines as foundation stock was of enormous benefit, so we could go on and breed true Akitas for generation after generation. My advice to novice owners is stop, look and listen. Talk to successful breeders, ask questions such as, how many litters and puppies did they breed to produce that one special dog? You might be amazed at the answer! Also a mega price does not ensure a mega dog – after all, I don't ever remember seeing an ugly puppy, but he or she is going to grow up fast and it could be into that graceful swan or the ugly duckling.

I cannot stress enough how important knowing the Standard of the breed is. Read it, learn it, memorise it and read it again; and finally, when you have made your decision and you are the proud owner of a sound, healthy puppy, make sure you socialise it to every noise, person, travel, etc., and ensure you finish up with a well-balanced, happy Akita – and good luck!!

BILL WYNN, *New Jersey, USA*
As a professional handler and breeder of the Bighorn Akitas, Bill answered the following questions.

Q. When did you first become involved with purebred dogs and what was the first breed of dog you owned?

A. I first became involved with pedigree dogs in 1969 when I worked with German Shepherds in the Obedience and K9 sections of the Police Department. Through this I was introduced to the Rottweiler and Dobermann. Dogs are known for their loyalty and the more I became involved, the more amazed I became by their intelligence. My German Shepherd was trained in police utility work as well as narcotics detection. Working and living with the dogs helps build a bond which cannot be broken. I was heavily involved with training all three breeds, the Rottweilers and Dobermanns in specialised fields and the German Shepherds in all-round utility work. I also became involved in breeding, importing some German Shepherds from Germany and purchasing others from some of the top US kennels of Gladys Taylor and Frank Lopez, who were also involved with police dogs. A few years after this my life in dogs changed for ever, when I first set eyes on an Akita. This dog was called Sachmo and from then on I

Bill Wynn handling a flashy red/white pinto –
Am. Ch. Bighorns Okane Of Kadai.

was hooked on the Akita breed.

Q. What made you decide to show and handle dogs and when did you become a professional handler?

A. As all my own experience was in training K9 narcotic dogs, I had my own show dogs professionally handled either by Sid Lamont or Walter Kuberski, whom I considered to be two of the best. Indeed, to this day, I consider Kuberski to be the best Rottweiler handler anywhere. At one show, (Farmington Valley K.C.), Sid

Lamont should have shown my Dobermann, Champ; however, this clashed with another of Sid's breeds so he persuaded me to take the dog in. I did and we won the class, or rather the dog did because he was a great dog, not because of anything I did. However, I really enjoyed being in the ring and started handling more and more. Once I became involved with the Akita, I handled all my own dogs, finishing many of our own breeding to their Championships. The more I won, the more I had requests to handle other people's dogs and it really evolved from there. It got to the point where I had so many clients that I needed an assistant and that is how June, my wife, became involved. We did, however, just handle Akitas, Rottweilers and German Shepherds, which kept us very busy.

Q. What breeds made your name as a handler, which do you prefer handling and when did you first handle an Akita?

A. I think first and foremost the Akita, whom we have been showing and breeding for about twenty years. Watching the grandchildren and great-grandchildren of your own stock win in the ring gives you a tremendous thrill. I have taken more Akitas to their title than any other breed.

Q. Which Akita do you consider to be the best you have handled and which, in your opinion, is the best you have seen?

A. A very tough question. The best one I have handled would be Am. Ch. SoHo's Black Star, but I am prejudiced because I bred him and June whelped him while I was on my way to the Akita National Specialty in Florida in 1985. I was showing Star at the same time that Am. Ch. The Widow Maker O'BJ and Am. Ch. Allure's Island Shogun were in the ring, and we had a great time head to head with all of them. As far as the best I have seen is concerned, I cannot mention just one dog. There have been many great dogs in one way or another and all in their own right. Having seen dogs from Sachmo, Widowmaker and Van Scoten Jones, and having the thrill of seeing Shogun win the National from the veteran class at Houston, and Return Of The Jedai with all his Best of Breeds at Westminster, I can appreciate the qualities of all these great dogs. However, probably the best Akita I ever saw was never in a show ring. This dog had everything – great head, tail set, top-line and a super mover, a perfect specimen of the breed, but no way could I talk the owner into showing him. To this day he is still a much loved family pet!

Q. Which kennel do you believe has had the greatest influence on the development of the breed?

A. In my opinion, three kennels had a tremendous influence on the breed, the Okii Yubi, O'BJ and Frerose kennels all produced some great dogs which remain in many pedigrees today.

Q. How important is it to you to get to know the Akitas you handle before showing them and would you normally pick up an Akita male 'cold' at the ringside?

A. It is always better to get to know the dogs you are going to handle, as they all have their own personalities and quirks. You need to decide which is the best way to set a particular dog up, or which is the best speed to gait him to get the best out of him for the judge. As many of the dogs are new to showing, we also have to get them used to being groomed and handled while other dogs are around. I try never to make it a practice of picking up a dog 'cold' as it is unlikely to perform well for someone it does not know. There are times when handlers will cover dogs for other handlers who may be in a conflicting ring with another breed, but usually the dog has been around the handler before and they are not total strangers.

Q. Do you feel the breed has improved over the years you have been handling a) in quality and b) in temperament?

A. As with any breed, the Akita has had its ups and downs as far as quality is concerned. For instance, rear ends were originally good, they then deteriorated, but are now improving again. There are times when the dogs seem to be better than the bitches and vice versa. One thing I do feel we are losing is type, and this is what sets the breed apart and makes it unique. Just because a dog moves well

does not mean it should win. First and foremost it has to look like an Akita, but unfortunately, this is not always the case. While the dogs that are winning are not good representatives of the breed, type will never improve. Many of the original Akitas were very tough, but over the years temperaments have improved, which is a good thing, as these dogs have to fit in with today's society and changing attitudes.

Q. Do you think that a quality dog with an owner/handler has as much chance of reaching the top in America as one shown by a professional handler?

A. As far as winning is concerned, the owner/handler has as much chance as the professional handler. Their biggest problem is time and money. To take a dog to the top in America, the dog must be out showing every single week, all year long. For an owner to do this is almost impossible, because of the amount of time which would be needed off work to allow for travelling and time spent at the shows. Money-wise it probably costs slightly less to employ a professional handler, as the expenses are divided between all the dogs which the handler carries. However, in the Akita ring, the owner/handler probably has as much chance as the professional, more than in most other breeds.

Q. If asked to give advice to a newcomer, what would you say helps to make a good handler?

A. To become a top handler you need to get to know your dog inside out, what makes him tick and what will show him off the best. Be patient and do not become discouraged if you do not win straightaway. Observe the professionals and study one whom you consider to be really good. Then practice at home with your own dog until you feel confident. The more you practice, the more secure you will feel the first time in the show ring. Never be afraid to ask questions of those more experienced in the breed, as most people are only too happy to help – and enjoy your dog showing!

MARGARET HIPPOLITE, Kodo Akitas, Nelson, New Zealand.

As one of New Zealand's first importers and a top breeder of the Akita, we asked Margaret Hippolite the following questions.

Q. When did you first become interested in purebred dogs and what was the first breed you owned and why?

A. My first dog was an Akita and I purchased her in 1989. I had always wanted a dog and when I saw an Akita on the Crufts TV special several years previously, it had been love at first sight. Why? Well I guess it's like why you pick your partner, because of a lot of things rolled into one and because you like the way they look too!

Q. When did you first buy an Akita and did you buy it as a show dog, foundation stock or just as a pet?

A. NZ. Ch. Sakura No Hana, or Shedo, came to live with us at one year old. Her sire was the well-known Am. Ch. The Real McCoy O'BJ of the USA. Her dam had been brought over from the UK in whelp by breeder Diane Murray of Sakura Kennels. I had spent several years waiting for the 'right Akita', so when I was offered a McCoy daughter, I could not have hoped for a better foundation. My next bitch was NZ. Ch. Gin Iro No Sakura. Koko, a McCoy grand-daughter, was the bitch that had more influence on my breeding programme and has consistently produced well.

Q. Who had the biggest influence on you in your first years in the breed and why?

A. As I read and collected anything and everything Akita, one obvious kennel stood out, the O'BJ Kennel of Bill and B.J. Andrews in the USA. Not only were their dogs consistently stunning, but they went on to produce puppies of the same quality or better. Dave and Jenny Killilea of the Redwitch Kennels in the UK had some lovely imports from the Goshen Kennels and I continue to appreciate their guidance and the bloodlines they entrusted me with. I also had friends closer to home in other breeds that taught me about dogs and dog breeding, giving me encouragement, advice and, at times, a fresh perspective. This has been and always will be invaluable to me.

101

NZ Ch. Redwitch High Hopes, owned by Margaret Hippolite.

Q. As a successful kennel yourself, what other Akita kennel do you most admire and why?

A. Obviously O'BJ for producing so many wonderful Akitas in the past and providing the breed with so many great foundations. In more recent times, Redwitch in the UK and Regalia in the USA. Both these kennels have produced consistently and have been rightfully awarded top honours in the show ring.

Q. Which dog and which bitch, that you have bred, do you consider to have contributed the most to your success as a breeder?

A. BITCH: NZ and Aus. Ch. Kodo Kreme de Koko – Peaches – because she epitomises the Akita to me and that, as a

breeder, is what I aim for. Since being exported to Australia in 1995, Peaches has taken Bitch Challenge Certificate at the Melbourne Royal and Bitch Challenge Certificate at the Victorian Akita Specialty every year, winning Best in Show at the Victorian Specialty this year, 1998, aged six-and-a-half years. Her sire is NZ Ch. Redwitch Secret Weapon, imported from the UK, and her dam is NZ Ch. Gin Iro No Sakura.

DOG: NZ Ch. Kodo Lone Star – Star – who has had an All Breeds Best in Show and is a consistent Group and In Show placer at All Breeds Championship Shows. He is from Sho 'n' Tel American Legend (an Am. Ch. Regalias Trans Action son), who was imported from the USA, and NZ Ch. Gin Iro No Sakura. To me, these two Akitas have proved that I can breed what I consider to be an Akita. The fact that so many well-respected judges from all parts of the world have also considered this to be so, by awarding them so highly and consistently in the show ring, has been an added honour.

Q. What is the most successful show dog you have owned or bred and what points do you attribute to his/her success?

A. Undoubtedly, Kiri, NZ Ch. Redwitch High Hopes. She is a dream to show and has a side gait that takes your breath away. Kiri has those important Akita characteristics – tight feet, triangular eyes, small, thick ears slightly rounded at the tips, tail set just right. Most importantly, she has 'presence'. At our largest dog show in New Zealand, the New Zealand Kennel Club National, Kiri has taken a Best of Group and also, the following year, Intermediate in Show. She is New Zealand's top winning Akita, having won three All Breeds, Best in Shows. These awards have been from well-respected judges from the USA and UK as well as our own New Zealand judges.

Q. When breeding, what do you consider to be the most important features of the breed?

A. Every feature that the Standard states is an important feature as far as I am concerned. One of my favourite quotes is "Type demands attention to detail, while balance combines these individual qualities so that a dog is not seen as a collection of parts." I think you must have the attention to detail – size and substance, those tight feet, correct, thick, treble coat, small, thick ear, slightly rounded at the tip – all the points that are printed in the Standard, but the real key is balance. This extends to balance in temperament as well. There is no point in having a magnificent Akita with unstable temperament. If we wish to preserve our breed and ensure its existence, then we must act responsibly and aim to breed Akitas with good, acceptable temperaments that we can live in harmony with.

Q. How important do you deem colour to be when picking a show puppy?

A. Again, you could apply the balance principle and another quote, "A good dog cannot be a bad colour." Colour can be used to your advantage to accentuate the positive.

Q. How much of your success do you put down to a) line breeding b) in-breeding and c) out-crossing?

A. I have used all three, but I would never out-cross without having a close line to go back into. Getting the mix is so important. I often see people import dogs, or include new bloodlines in their breeding programmes, only to breed so intensely back into what they had that they may as well not have bothered. Pedigrees have a strong influence on my breeding programme.

Q. What points do you think contributed to making your kennel so successful and what advice would you give to a newcomer in the breed?

A. Commitment and determination spring to mind, then there is passion, patience and love for my dogs. Being over the other side of the world made accessing the bloodlines I admire extremely difficult. I researched thoroughly and am still learning, keeping up to date. I have been fortunate to have support from people in the breed whom I greatly admire and who have become close friends. These people are very important to me as friends and have had a major influence on the success of my kennel. For a newcomer, know what you want, set goals, make plans and focus on achieving them. Your programme may have to be flexible, as nature does not always go to plan, but at least do have one. Most importantly, enjoy your Akitas and treasure the breed.

DAVID KILLILEA, Redwitch Akitas West Yorkshire.
As top breeder in the UK for the last seven years, the following questions were put to David.

Q. When did you first become interested in purebred dogs and what was the first breed you owned and why?

A. I was brought up with German Shepherd dogs and working sheepdogs on the farm, but the first pedigree show dog I owned was a British Bulldog. I had first seen the breed while at an agricultural show handling pedigree bulls and immediately fell in love with them. My first Bulldog was purchased from Les Lund of Qualco Bulldogs about thirty years ago, he is now secretary of the Manchester Championship Dog Show. My first successful show dog was from the famous Foresquare kennel of Penny Shore and was called Foresquare Gold Dust. This bitch was very successful as a puppy and basically got me hooked on the dog show scene.

Q. When did you first buy an Akita and did you buy it as a show dog, as foundation stock or just as a pet?

A. My first Akita was purchased in 1983 from Brett Cassidy of the Littlecreek Kennels and surprisingly we remain friends to this day! At the time, she was the only puppy available from the second litter to be born in quarantine in this country and, although not oozing breed type, she was sound, had 0-0 hips and a clear eye certificate. Bred to Am. Ch. The Real McCoy, she produced some typy puppies. But it was to the Overhill Kennel of Meg Purnell-Carpenter that I turned, to purchase my foundation stock in the form of Overhill's Marlow's Miracle and Overhill's Lizzie's Girl, who were by O'BJ Aces High and Am. Ch. Sachette No Okii Yubis, both imports from the famous O'BJ kennel.

Q. Who had the biggest influence on you in your first years in the breed and why?

A. This has to be Bill and B.J. Andrews of the O'BJ Kennel. In the early days there was no-one in this country with sufficient knowledge of the breed to be able to guide newcomers and it was only through meeting the American breeders and handlers that we could begin to learn about the Akita. Meeting Bill and B.J. in January 1985 at the National Specialty had a tremendous influence on me, and seeing the type of Akita they were producing gave me the incentive and determination to produce that quality of type in this country. There were, however, other people whom I met in those early days who were of great help and encouragement to me, and to this day remain great friends and very special people, namely Catherine and Charlie Bell and Ed Finnegan Jnr.

Q. As a very successful kennel yourself, what other Akita kennel do you most admire and why?

A. Probably the Goshen Kennel of Lew and Julie Hoehn of Indiana, USA for their honesty and integrity in their dealings with us when allowing us to purchase some of the finest Akitas this country has ever seen, not only as show dogs but as prolific sires and dams. The other kennel in the USA which I greatly admire, although I have never had dealings with them, is the Koma Inu Kennel of Judythe Dunne. This kennel consistently produces type, soundness and superb heads. Maybe we can get together one day! As far as Britain is concerned, I think mention should be made of the progress the Keskai Kennel of Sue and

David with his pride and joy – Ch. Am. Ch. Goshens Heir Apparent At Redwitch.

Kevin Sadler has made over the past five years, producing an increasing amount of typy and sound Akitas.

Q. Which dog and which bitch, that you have bred, do you consider to have contributed the most to your success as a breeder?

A. Without doubt, Ch. Lizda Zee Zee Flash has left the greatest legacy. As the top producing bitch to date, giving us Ch. Nor. Ch. Redwitch Dancin' in the Dark, together with three other Champions, Zee was also a super, stylish show girl and our first-ever Akita to take a Group placement. She was also the first British-bred Champion bitch in this country. As far as dogs are concerned, I would rather answer this in two parts. As a breeder, it has to be Ch. Nor. Ch. Redwitch Dancin' in the Dark who, although only having been back in this country for a short time, has proved himself to be a very dominant sire, producing no less than five different Challenge Certificate winners in 1998 to date. Although we were only lucky enough to own him, I cannot answer this question without mentioning Ch. Goshens Heir Apparent at Redwitch. A dog of this magnitude probably only passes through your kennel once in a lifetime. We are truly grateful for the time we had with Prince and for the tremendous influence he stamped on the breed in this country. He was very, very special.

Q. Which is the most successful show dog you have owned or bred and what points do you attribute to his success?

A. It has to be Ch. Nor. Ch. Redwitch Dancin' in the Dark. For the first three years of his life he dominated the Akita rings in Norway, winning everything from Best in Show at the Club Show on his debut as a baby, to Groups and Best in Show All Breeds. Since his return to the UK he has totally dominated the Akita ring and the Utility Group taking every award there is to take. We believe his type and soundness have contributed most to his success, appealing both to breed specialists and all-rounders, the like of which has never been seen before in the breed. His glamour and showmanship are second to none, and although not the easiest dog to handle, when the chips are down he always pulls out all the stops.

Q. When breeding, what do you consider to be the most important features of the breed?

A. It has to be overall breed type – without this you do not have an Akita and this is what stands him out from the crowd. Although soundness plays a close second, it is quality and type that make a breed what it is. There are plenty of dogs which are sound and typy, but there are only a few great dogs which ooze breed type and are sound. Whether you are lucky enough to own them, breed them or just see them, when the hairs on the back of your neck and arms stand up, what you are looking at is a true Akita.

Q. How important do you deem colour

to be when picking a show puppy?

A. This is probably the last thing I look for. First and foremost, I look for type and soundness and for the puppy which stands out from the rest, whether it be male or female. If this is the brilliant red and white then all the better, but if it is a fawn, then a fawn puppy is what we will keep. I have seen many successful kennels built on type, but I have seen many others go downhill while trying to breed for colour alone.

Q. How much of your success do you put down to
a) line breeding
b) in breeding
c) out-crossing?

A. The success of the Redwitch Kennel is due entirely to line breeding. Although this was very difficult in the early days, and other options would have been far easier and less expensive, we were determined to stick to our guns and try and produce a type which was instantly recognisable and fitted the Breed Standard. Although there have been times when we have needed to use an outcross, we have done this with the utmost care,

ensuring that the outcross was also line-bred in his own lines.

Q. What points do you think contributed to making your kennel so successful and what advice would you give to a newcomer in the breed?

A. I feel the success of this kennel is due mainly to the fact that we both work together, having the same goals and the same high standards. Our love for the Akita has given us the determination to carry on, even in the face of adversity – never wearing rose-coloured spectacles and even at times, being critical of the best of our own dogs. The best advice I can give to anyone coming into the breed is to take a long look at the top kennels, decide which type pleases you, and do not rush into any purchases. Watch, listen and learn and do not be swayed by the gossips. Before you can be successful at winning, you have to learn to lose gracefully. Very few people are lucky enough to get that very special show dog first time round. Success does not come easy, it has to be worked at. Never lose sight of the fact that the greatest pleasure is owning an Akita in the first place.

9 BREEDING AKITAS

Looking back to when the breed was first introduced to the United Kingdom in the early eighties, the original imports were purchased with very little knowledge or experience of the Akita by the first breeders. The honesty and integrity of the Americans had to be relied upon, and whereas many were and still are to this day, extremely helpful and honest with their dealings, without doubt there were those who off-loaded and made a quick dollar with little regard to the damage it could do to the small gene pool in the UK. There were also those in Britain who rushed to purchase with little regard to type and quality, to satisfy a buoyant, expensive puppy market.

So many of the early breedings were done with no real thought to planning or suitability. A mixture of problems – type, temperament, soundness and heredity – sprang up from all different directions, and only a few dedicated enthusiasts made early progress in the breed. Interestingly, most of these are still with us today.

PEDIGREES AND PLANNING

There is no doubt that the Redwitch kennel has been the most successful Akita kennel to date in the UK and our sires have been the top producers year in and year out. Whereas newcomers to the breed today can ask for help from various successful kennels, we had to rely on books, pedigrees and a thorough understanding of the Breed Standard.

Our decision to follow one tightly in-bred line and one very influential sire is well-known. However, this decision was based purely on the quality of the type that we saw; the importance of the pedigrees is something we have learned over the years. From our own experience, and having watched the downfall of other kennels who have bred willy-nilly, we feel the Akita is a breed which has to be closely line-bred continually to produce type and quality. Unlike some breeds, for example the Bulldog, where the possibility of success from any form of outcrossing is high, the Akita must have stability in the pedigree or the breeder will pay the

Ed Finnegan Jnr with the greatest of them all: Am. Ch. Okii Yubi's Sachmo Of Makoto.

The third top-producing sire of all time in the US: Am. Ch. O'BJ Bigson Of Sachmo. Owned by Bill and B.J. Andrews.

penalty and lose type. The use of an outcross sire may be needed occasionally, to inject colour or replace something you may have lost, but this sire must himself be tightly line-bred within his own lines, and his progeny should be carefully checked first to ensure he can produce what you are looking for.

When planning a breeding, careful thought should first be given as to whether you are doing it for the right reasons. Thankfully, gone are the days when Akita puppies sold for silly money, and, with the advent of the Dangerous Dogs Act, the larger, guarding breeds are not as popular with the general public as they were, so quite often a litter of puppies may not all be sold by the time

Am. Mex. Int. Ch. Koma-Inu Made In The USA: Quality breeding at its best. Bred by Judythe Dunn.   Ashbey Photography.

Pedigree of Ch. Goshens Dark 'N' Debonaire At Redwitch

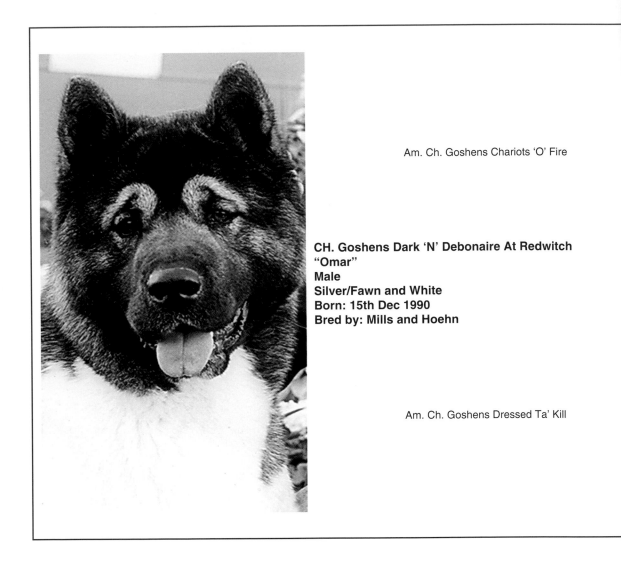

Am. Ch. Goshens Chariots 'O' Fire

**CH. Goshens Dark 'N' Debonaire At Redwitch
"Omar"
Male
Silver/Fawn and White
Born: 15th Dec 1990
Bred by: Mills and Hoehn**

Am. Ch. Goshens Dressed Ta' Kill

they reach eight weeks of age. Do you have the facilities to run them on if not? Whereas one cheeky eight-week-old is a bundle of fun, seven running around the back garden at sixteen weeks can be both very messy and very expensive.

Having made the decision to breed, carefully study both your bitch and her pedigree. Decide which of her faults you need to correct and what are her virtues.

Am. Ch. O'BJ Kings Ransom

Am. Ch. The Widow Maker O'BJ
Am. Ch. The Real McCoy O'BJ
Am. Ch. The Same Dame O'BJ

Am. Ch. The Mad Hatter O'BJ
Am. Ch. Daijobu's Joto
Am. Ch. O'BJ Nikki No Nikki

Am. Ch. The Dames On Target O'BJ

Am. Ch. The Real McCoy O'BJ
Am. Ch. Okii Yubi's Sachmo Of Makoto
Am. Ch. O'BJ Miss Taken Tiger De Alicia

Am. Ch. The Same Dame O'BJ
Am. Ch. Kakwa's Orca
Am. Ch. O'BJ Dame Of The Game

Am. Ch. O'BJ Kings Ransom

Am. Ch. The Widow Maker O'BJ
Am. Ch. The Real McCoy O'BJ
Am. Ch. The Same Dame O'BJ

Am. Ch. The Mad Hatter O'BJ
Am. Ch. Daijobu's Joto
Am. Ch. O'BJ Nikki No Nikki

Am. Ch. Kinouks Dream Maker

Am. Ch. Tarmalanes Kuma Yama Khan
Am. Ch. Akita Tani's Daimyo
Am. Ch. Frerose's Sarah Lei

Am. Ch. Kinouks Flower Child
Am. Ch. Okii Yubi's Sachmo Of Makoto
Am. Ch. Kinouks Kor-I

With these in mind, decide what you want from the sire, whether it be type, colour, coat, etc. Having made a short list, take a long look at the progeny that has been produced, particularly to similarly bred bitches. Most of all, ensure the dog is dominant in the parts you are looking for. Occasionally, a dog of superb breed type may not be a dominant sire and is not capable of reproducing his type, yet his

Typical of the Koma-Inu kennel, and a double grandson, Ch. Koma-Inu Bronze Bruin was not only a top show dog, he was also a top producer.

Another product of quality breeding, shown here at seven months. Redwitch Secret Love Of Claran was sired by Ch. Am. Ch. Goshens Heir Apparent At Redwitch out of Ch. Goshens Classy Sassy At Redwitch. Photo: Dalton.

Right: The first Akita to be sent by the Redwitch kennel to the USA, he gained his title within two weeks on the Florida circuit. Am. Ch. Redwitch Billy Bigtime (Aust. Ch. Jack Daniels At Redwitch – Redwitch Forbidden Secret At Jocolda) is owned by Bill and June Wynn.

litter brother, although not of quite the same quality, may be a more dominant producer.

Everyone's goal is to produce a better puppy and that special show prospect. Nevertheless, after studying both pedigrees and sires, there are times that, although on paper it should work, for some reason certain breedings do not 'click'. If this happens, do not be disheartened, but choose a different sire and try again. However, if on the second attempt, things still do not turn out right, you should seriously be looking at your own bitch, no matter how good her quality, and questioning whether she is capable of reproducing as good or better than herself. Too many breeders go on, year after year, using their own bitches and their own stud dogs, never improving the quality of what they have. You should be capable of taking your head out of the sand and recognising quality consistently produced by other kennels and be prepared to go out and buy that special puppy and start again.

Once you have purchased that exciting prospect, do not fall back into the same trap of using your own stud dog again or your friend's up the road. Be prepared to travel hundreds of miles if necessary to obtain the services of a top line-bred

Northlands Embers At Dawn, aged 12 weeks. The product of half Japanese, half American breeding. Note those fabulous thick, rounded ears and the truly Oriental expression. Bred and owned by Loren and Christina Egland.

The ultimate in Redwitch breeding to date: Ch. Nor. Ch. Redwitch Dancin' In The Dark. Runner-up Top Dog All Breeds 1997, breed recordholder, multi all-breed BIS winner and Top Stud Dog 1998.

Photo: Carol Ann Johnson.

From the very first Redwitch litter, and after a successful show career in England, Redwitch The Standard Bearer went on to become the first Akita to win BIS All Breeds at Nantes, France, 1990.

producer. One other tip, always pay the stud fee and never exchange it for the pick of litter, as this may just be the super star you have been waiting for. Surely that is what you have been breeding for in the first place?

HEALTH AND SUITABILITY

Along with studying pedigrees and the type of the breeding pair, you should also be checking the health of these lines. One important factor is hips. While not wishing to become obsessed with hip scores to the detriment of the rest of the dog, this is something which should always be taken into consideration. The breed average currently stands at around twelve, and whereas a 0-0 score is very satisfying, this is of no consequence on an untypical Akita. A dog with a 6-6 score

who can reproduce type is of far more benefit to the breed.

Another factor for consideration is eyes, and whereas the Akita as a breed does not currently suffer many eye problems, each dog should also have been checked under some recognised veterinary authority such as the British Veterinary Association (BVA) Eye Scheme or the Canine Eye Registration Foundation (CERF) in the US.

Hopefully, several of the puppies you hope to breed will go to good pet homes in a family environment where they will live for the rest of their lives. For this reason, temperament should be on top of your list of priorities. When choosing your stud dog, no excuse for bad temperament should be made. While the mature Akita male is allowed to be macho, aloof or standoffish, he is on no account allowed to show aggression toward people.

Something else to consider where a male Akita is kept in a family pet situation is whether it is worth allowing this male to be used at stud, for what might be a one-off occasion. Although this should not affect his temperament as such, it could well affect his social and territorial habits. Whereas the daily walk was always a pleasure, it could become a game of tug-of-war as he spends his time with his nose glued to the ground sniffing where bitches have possibly been in season. The same consideration should be given as to the suitability of breeding a bitch who is a much-loved pet. People are often wrongly advised to let a bitch have a litter; as a family pet there is no need for this. She can be safely spayed after her first season, which will not only remove the problems related to bitches in season, but will also eliminate the risk of "ladies'" problems later in life.

BREEDING YOUR BITCH

Having decided to breed your bitch and carefully chosen your stud dog, thought must now be given as to the time of year and how it fits in with your daily life. Your bitch should normally have two seasons per year, so choose the time which best suits your plans. Have you got holidays booked? Do you want winter puppies who will possibly be with you over the Christmas period? This is also not the best time to be selling puppies.

Once all these decisions have been made, it is important to watch your bitch carefully so that you know on which day her season started. Write this date on the calendar so that you do not forget, and advise the owner of the stud dog so that they are aware of roughly what day to expect you. You should also enquire as to whether there are facilities to keep your bitch for a few days, or if there is somewhere close by where you can stay if it is necessary to do two matings and you have a long way to travel. From the stud dog's owner's point of view, there is nothing worse than the phone ringing and the voice at the other end saying 'My bitch is in season and it needs breeding tonight!'. You will be given more care and consideration if everything is planned carefully and the stud dog in question has not been double-booked.

From the first day of her season, check your bitch daily. Whereas we would normally expect to breed a bitch between her eleventh and fifteenth days, an Akita bitch can breed as early as her fifth and as late as her twenty-fourth day. Watch for the obvious changes, the colour of her blood-loss going from bright red to a watery pinkish-brown. This is not easy, as an Akita bitch will clean herself up as fast as she makes a mess. Watch for her vulva swelling and that tell-tale sign of her tail flagging from side to side while being handled around her hindquarters. If you are lucky enough to own a male dog also, you can quite easily use him as a tester, although obviously ensuring that the two do not get together. However, you may prefer to have a swab or blood test done by your vet, which should tell you if she is ready for breeding and when she will ovulate.

THE MATING

Once the correct day is ascertained, you need to ensure that your bitch's day is as stress-free as possible. If it is during hot weather, try to arrange an evening mating, which will be better both for her and for the stud dog. On arrival at your destination, make sure she is on a lead and has the opportunity to relieve herself and empty her bowels before being introduced to the dog. It is advisable to let them get to know each other while both are on leads and under supervision. You will soon know whether the bitch is receptive to the dog. We always do all our breedings under close supervision to avoid any accidents, either damage to the stud dog or to the bitch. We normally support the bitch underneath and hold her head while giving her reassurance. If everything is as it should be, the bitch will stand firm for the dog and the breeding should take place naturally. A good stud dog will not mess about, but will get on with his job, with a minimal amount of fuss.

There is the odd occasion, particularly in the case of a bitch which is very much a family pet, where although everything appears to be as it should be and her rear end says 'OK', her head definitely says 'NO!'. On these occasions, the use of a muzzle is advisable while the actual mating is taking place. Once the dogs have tied and been turned, the bitch will normally settle and the muzzle may be removed.

If the mating is successful and everything goes according to plan, then one breeding is ideal, as even if she ovulates within the next twenty-four hours, the sperm will still be live. However, if you feel that the mating was slightly early and you would rather repeat it, this should be done forty-eight hours later. It is advisable to get a stud receipt with confirmation of a repeat mating, should this first one be unsuccessful.

You should now take your bitch home and keep her reasonably quiet and relaxed. Keep her away from any other males, particularly until you are quite sure her season has finished.

For those of you who own a stud dog which is used on a regular basis, it is important to keep an eye on him and check for any discharge or sign of infection, as this can easily be transmitted when a mating takes place.

CONCEPTION TO WHELPING

For the first few weeks of pregnancy you will not notice any visible sign of change other than, maybe, a change in her mannerisms. She may become a little quieter, or possibly more affectionate towards her immediate family. From twenty-eight days you could have her palpated by a vet or scanned to see if she is in whelp, or you can just sit back with bated breath and hope to see her bloom as her pregnancy proceeds. At around five weeks there should be a noticeable difference to her rear nipples which should be protruding and pink. By six weeks she should be really blooming and have quite a little pot-belly. It is at this stage that her food should be increased, so she is getting half as much again of her normal daily ration. It should, however, be divided into at least two meals. Overfeeding too early, or to extremes, can cause overly large puppies, which are a problem for the bitch to pass.

The normal gestation time for a bitch is sixty-three days. However, all breeds tend to differ and we have found, through experience, that most Akitas will whelp down at fifty-nine days and sometimes as early as fifty-seven.

You should be thoroughly organised before this time, knowing where you are going to whelp your bitch, and have her settled into her new quarters at least a few days before the due date. If you have never whelped a bitch before, or have whelped some of the more complicated breeds, with a bit of luck you are about to see nature at its best.

An Akita bitch in labour, panting heavily.

Whelping is over, and the mother is happily settled nursing her puppies.

Twenty-four hours after whelping: The Akita bitch will cope with all her puppies' needs, feeding them and cleaning them.

GIVING BIRTH

The first sign that things are starting to happen will probably be your bitch 're-arranging' her bed. By this time she should be safely settled in a whelping box of which the ideal size for an Akita is four feet by four feet. At this stage there is little point giving her clean, quality bedding as she will only shred it, so newspaper is ideal, as she can rip this up and arrange it as she wants and it will also help to soak up the fluids she passes. No two bitches whelp down the same and whereas some can be in slow labour for twenty-four to forty-eight hours, others can whelp within an hour or so of showing the first signs,

so close supervision is recommended.

Most Akita bitches will pant quite heavily while in labour before the onset of contractions. Once these start the next stage will be the bitch starting to push and her waters breaking. You will normally expect the first puppy to be born within an hour or two of this happening. Most Akita bitches whelp down very easily and can cope very well (although we always supervise) and it is very rare to find an Akita who does not make a natural mother. Puppies are normally born within one to three hours of each other, so as long as your bitch does not look distressed or is not pushing for long periods without

Within the first two days, the puppies should be checked for dewclaws on the hindlegs.

results, there is no need to panic. Depending on the size of the litter, whelping can take from just a couple of hours up to ten or twelve.

Always keep note of whether an afterbirth appears with each puppy and it is also advisable to have an injection given by your vet at the end of delivery to clear out any debris which may be left in your bitch. If there is a long gap between whelpings and the bitch has already had three or four puppies, we always make sure that they are put onto the bitch to feed. This both helps to bring her milk down and also often starts the contractions again.

When she has finished whelping and has settled down with her puppies, after checking they are all feeding alright, we try to leave the bitch with a minimum of interference and fuss, as she needs to bond with her babies. The following day we normally wash her rear end off to make her feel more comfortable and line the whelping box with a quality fleece bedding pad. Although Akitas would normally shred any bedding into two-inch squares within minutes, it is interesting that while nursing puppies, the Akita bitch will rarely tear up her bed.

Within the first two days, you should check for dewclaws on the rear legs. Although not commonly seen on an Akita, occasionally puppies are born with them, so these should be removed. Apart from this, the first three weeks are relatively easy. An Akita mother normally keeps her puppies spotlessly clean and, apart from changing her bedding and feeding her, you should interfere as little as possible. We also continue with two feeds per day while a bitch is nursing puppies and naturally, clean water is always readily available.

REARING

By the age of three weeks, the puppies are usually up on their feet and getting about and are ready for a little bit extra in the way of nourishment. There are different schools of thought on feeding puppies and there are other successful alternatives, but we can only advise on our own methods. We have found that feeding

A week old: the puppies will divide their time between eating and sleeping.

quality complete foods to Akita puppies rears them extremely well, bringing them along slowly and producing the bone and substance at the required age. We start them off on one meal per day for a couple of days, with the food soaked down to gruel. We then increase to two meals for a couple of days, then three, and by the time they are four weeks, they are well into a routine of four meals per day. At the same time, we gradually soak the food less and less so that the pups are taking it formed but soft. Fresh, clean water is always available – we never give milk.

By this time the puppies are becoming individual characters and are getting about and play-fighting, so they need more room than just the whelping box. We try to have them in a pen where they can get out and about a little and also where the bitch can get away from them for short periods, as by now they are demanding and the milk teeth are like needles. At around five weeks we start taking her away from them in the daytime and putting her back at night; before they are six weeks old they are weaned completely.

Puppies should be wormed regularly with a gentle wormer, starting at three weeks, then five and seven weeks. We also worm the mother at this time. We normally find the pups wean off their mother without any fuss, and once

weaned, we do not allow the bitch back in to them even though she may appear very heavy with milk. We normally cut her food down for a couple of days and increase her exercise, which not only helps to dry her up, but helps to take her mind off the puppies.

The growth rate of an Akita puppy from three weeks to seven weeks is tremendous, so much so that sometimes you would swear they had grown overnight, so a watchful eye should be kept on the food intake. Puppies' motions are a good sign of how they are; if these are well-formed but soft, they are usually digesting their food and taking sufficient. Too much will give loose motions. A good guide on how your pup is doing is to look down over the back – if there is a nice rounded rib cage with just a slight hint of a waistline behind, this is correct. Too much weight on a puppy is bad for the bone structure; but not enough weight will fail to produce a good spring of rib.

We continue with four meals per day until our pups are around twelve weeks, then cut one feed out, but increase the others proportionately. This continues until around five months, when we start feeding two meals per day, and at around eleven to twelve months we put them on to one meal. However, some people prefer to always feed twice per day.

Feeding time: The first solid meal, offered at three weeks, proves an instant success.

10 *BREED ASSOCIATED CONDITIONS*

This chapter is not written to frighten you or dissuade you from owning an Akita. In general, the Akita as a breed is exceptionally healthy, probably more so than many others. However, as with any breed, there are specific, related problems which can appear from time to time, although fortunately these are very rare.

The most important point is to draw everyone's attention to the fact that, through no-one's fault, these conditions can occasionally occur and it is through sharing knowledge and experiences that we will better learn to cope, should the need arise. Regular screening and careful breeding practices – that is breeding from dogs known to be free from genetic disorders – will help to minimise or eliminate many of these problems.

ENTROPION

Thankfully far less common nowadays than when the breed was first introduced into the UK, entropion is a turning-in of the eye rim, allowing the lashes to scratch across the eyeball, ultimately resulting in ulceration and possible perforation of the cornea. The lower lid is more commonly affected although, occasionally, the upper lid shows signs also. Symptoms are runny eyes and irritation causing the dog to rub its head with the front paws. Surgical correction is usually very successful, although this is not normally undertaken until after six months of age to allow for changes in bone structure. Dogs that have undergone this surgery are barred from competition in the conformation ring. If left untreated, serious cases can lead to severe ulceration and ultimately, total blindness. This is an hereditary problem and affected stock should not be bred from.

ECTROPION

This is the reverse of entropion, with the bottom lid sagging outwards and downwards, exposing the conjunctiva and cornea. Although more unsightly than uncomfortable, this condition does expose the eye to dirt and foreign objects and so ultimately can lead to infection.

PROGRESSIVE RETINAL ATROPHY (PRA)

This is a genetic disorder causing degeneration of the sensory retinal cells which line the back of the eyeball and leading, eventually, to total blindness.

Although tests can detect problems quite early in life, this condition does not normally become apparent until the dog is mature, very often as late as four or five years old. It is also thought to be a simple recessive disorder, meaning that while a dog will show no signs of the problem, it may be passed on to its puppies.

Very often, dogs are used in breeding programmes many times before being identified as carriers. There are eye-testing schemes available using qualified specialist vets.

Akitas can now be screened by this means, and this test is repeated each year. However, the certificate signifies that the eye is clear at the time of examination only, and symptoms can develop later.

Breeders should also note that litter brothers and sisters of afflicted dogs may also carry the disease.

It is, however, worth bearing in mind that a blind dog which is otherwise very healthy, can live a long and happy life in its own known environment.

MICROPHTHALMIA

Otherwise known as 'small eye', this problem can be detected in puppies almost as soon as the eye opens. The smaller than usual eye is often cloudy and unresponsive to light and can be accompanied by cataracts. Both parents of affected puppies are carriers, as can be litter brothers or sisters, so they should not be used for breeding purposes in the future.

HIP DYSPLASIA

This condition is covered in more detail by Dr Malcolm Willis in the following chapter but, briefly, it can affect either one or both of the hip joints, and occurs when the ball joint is pulled away from the socket to a lesser or greater degree. Depending on the severity, symptoms are limping and stiffness, particularly when rising, and pain, although this is not easily detectable in an Akita.

There are Hip Dysplasia Schemes available. The tests involved give an excellent guide as to the state of your Akita's hips and all stock should be X-rayed before breeding. Causes for hip dysplasia can be anything from over-feeding or over-exercising as a puppy to trauma or inheritance.

PANOSTEITIS

This is an inherited, congenital disorder seen most frequently in the large, heavy-boned breeds which experience accelerated growth spurts, including the Akita. It is caused by the bone growing faster than the surrounding tissue, so that the membrane which covers and forms new bone is torn away from the existing bone, also causing ligament problems. Normally affecting your stock between six to fifteen months, symptoms are limping, favouring of one or more paws or legs and occasionally swelling of limbs. The condition requires treatment to relieve inflammation of the membrane and ligaments, but most dogs will then outgrow the condition by the time they have finished their growth spurts.

SKIN DISORDERS

Again, this is something that was a real problem when the breed was first imported, with many lines suffering from skin complaints which varied from a pink rash to weeping sores and coat loss. Whether these problems were mainly food-related and, as breeders have learned more about the correct feeding and nourishment of the Akita, we have helped to eradicate many of them, is hard to tell, but we certainly do not see such a high incidence of dogs suffering from skin complaints as we used to.

Occasionally, you may see puppies with what can only be described as nappy (diaper) rash. This may be due to a reaction to airborne pollutants on wet grass, rubbing across the underbelly which is still very low to the ground at this stage. Some types of disinfectant, household cleaners and carpet fresheners can also have the same effect.

The type of food you give your Akita can have a tremendous effect on the skin and coat. Some feeds contain high levels of cereal which can cause 'hot spots'. The reaction to these can vary from itching to pimples, coat loss and eczema. Constant licking and scratching will then exaggerate the problem. If your Akita suffers any of the aforementioned, it is worth checking the contents of your current food supply and maybe you should consider changing it for a couple of weeks to see if this eliminates the problem.

MANGE

There are two types of mange, sarcoptic and demodectic, both of which require immediate veterinary attention. Sarcoptic mange is caused by a mite which is invisible to the naked eye, burrowing into the skin causing intense irritation and frantic scratching. Transmittable from dog to dog, it commonly affects under the forelegs, the thighs and the edge of the ears. It can also live on humans for a short time causing irritating spots.

The mite causing demodectic mange is a normal inhabitant of the hair follicles on most dogs and is harmless for most of the time. Whether as a result of stress, or for some other reason, these mites can suddenly cause a reaction which varies in intensity. Dermatitis and hair loss, possibly around the head or feet, are often the earliest signs and while it may remain localised, it can erupt all over the body.

All of the above skin disorders can be debilitating for a time, but they are all treatable and your Akita should soon resume good health. However, it may be that the onset of skin problems signifies a more serious health problem.

AUTO-IMMUNE DISORDERS
These develop when the immune system makes a mistake and produces antibodies to the body's own tissues. Quite why this happens is not known, but a combination of a genetically inherited predisposition which is triggered off by environmental factors, e.g. viruses or drugs, may be the reason.

VKH (VOGT-KOYANAGI-HARADA)
Otherwise known as Harada's disease, this terrible illness has been identified in Akitas. Symptoms will normally present themselves between fifteen months to two years and include sores or scabs on the nose, lips and genitals, cloudy and bloodshot eyes, loss of pigmentation and eventual hair loss. Dogs may also exhibit behavioural problems and/or head tilt. Affected dogs will eventually go blind. Early diagnosis, although not easy, is essential to enable any sort of success in treatment. In many cases, an auto-immune thyroid disease may also be diagnosed.

PEMPHIGUS FOLIACEUS (PF)
This skin problem occurs when the immune system begins manufacturing antibodies against the dog's own skin, attempting to reject it as if it were a foreign body.

Red spots first appear, quickly turning into blisters and then forming crusts on the nose, ears, around the eyes and on the pads of the feet. In serious cases these crusts may cover much of the body. Other symptoms include loss of pigment, lethargy, stiff joints and even lameness.

It normally occurs in mature dogs, although it can appear at any age, again it is often associated with auto-immune thyroid disease.

AUTO-IMMUNE THYROID DISEASE AND HYPOTHYROIDISM
An auto-immune disease whereby antibodies are set up to destroy the body's own thyroid gland, slowly destroying the tissues over a number of years and leading to a reduction in the production of thyroid hormones and resulting in hypothyroidism.

Symptoms vary and dogs can show one or many of them, including skin disorders varying from hair loss to seborrhea or bacterial skin infections, lethargy, obesity, muscle or nerve weakness and infertility.

If your Akita displays any of the above problems it is essential you consult your vet immediately. No dog suffering from any auto-immune disorder, should be used for breeding.

11

GENETICS AND THE AKITA
By Dr Malcolm B. Willis

The Akita like every other dog has descended from some form of wolf and has the same number of chromsosomes as the wolf, namely 78, or more accurately, 39 pairs. The cells of the body number millions and each will contain in its nucleus the 39 pairs. The exception is in germ cells – sperm and ova – which carry only one member of each of the 39 pairs. Thus when sperm and ova unite at conception the new animal carries the 39 pairs once more with half of its chromosomes coming from each parent.

Old ideas that sires give specific traits and dams contribute others are without foundation. Clearly one parent may give a better set of genes to its offspring than the other and thus have a seemingly greater input for good but every dog has 50% of its genes in common with its parents and also with its siblings.

GENETIC MAKE-UP
Genes are an integral part of each chromosome and are made up of DNA. Genes are always found at a specific location(or locus) on a specific chromosome but may be of different forms called alleles. Some genes have many alternative alleles while others have only two or, in some breeds no alternatives.

For example the gene M (alternative m) gives rise to the greyish merle colour seen in many sheepdog breeds. The Akita has the merle 'gene' but does not have the version causing merle colour (M) but rather its alternative m or non-merle. Since each dog must have two of each gene (having derived one from each parent) all Akitas are mm and thus homozygous for mm or non merle. When breeding Akitas, the merle gene does not come into the issue because all Akitas are mm at this particular locus.

In contrast, at the B locus Akitas can have either B or b. The allele B allows black pigment to form in the dog and the alternative b prevents black pigment. With two different genes there are three different genotypes (genetic combinations) namely BB, Bb or bb. However, B is a dominant allele in that it acts even if present in a single dose whereas b is a recessive allele operating only when present in duplicate. Thus BB and Bb both allow black pigment to form and are thus identical in phenotype (outward appearance) whereas bb gives rise to no black pigment and is a distinct phenotype.

Because a dog carries B does not mean that it will be black in colour but it will carry black pigment so it will have a black nose and lips, for example, even if it is a white dog. In contrast, the bb individual cannot form black pigment and is going to have a liver or brown nose and will have no black pigment anywhere.

INHERITANCE OF COAT
Whether an allele is recessive or dominant does not affect its 'value' to the dog but it will affect what happens in breeding. Very few defects or anomalies are dominant, because if something is dominant it can be seen and thus affected dogs can be discarded. In contrast a defect that is recessive can be carried by a dog without the owner being aware of this.

For example, the Akita is not a long-coated breed but long coats do occur. In all breeds the long coat version is recessive so that we have L (short coat) and l (long coat). Dogs that are LL or

Ll are short-coated and those that are ll are long-coated. Mating long-coated dogs together gives rise to 100% long coats because one is mating ll to ll and, obviously, no other alternatives exist. However, mating short-coated dogs can give rise to various combinations including long coats but only in specific instances. Mating LL to LL will give rise to 100% LL offspring, but mating LL to Ll will also give rise to 100% short-coated offspring but half of them will be carriers (Ll) and the breeder may be totally unaware of this. Long coats usually arise when the breeder mates two carriers without perhaps being aware that the animals were indeed carriers. Thus Ll to Ll would give rise to 25% LL, 50% Ll and 25% ll, and thus a ratio of three short coats to each long coat.

Obviously these percentages will apply to large numbers and not to a specific litter where numbers born may not be divisible by four, and where chance may not give the exact ratio expected. Many long coat carriers that are Ll may not be identified because they were always mated to LL partners or because, by chance, the ll did not crop up when Ll animals were mated. However, widely-used stud dogs which are Ll are likely to be identified.

INHERITED DEFECTS
Long coat is not a biological defect that is harmful to the dog and is thus of minor importance but there are several

defects in the Akita which are inherited in similar fashion to long coat and which are serious. These include:

DEAFNESS: Dogs are born deaf in one or both ears and the condition is often associated with white colour, especially on the head.

PRIMARY GLAUCOMA: Dogs have fluid pressure in the eye leading to pain and blindness.

PROGRESSIVE RETINAL ATROPHY (PRA): This condition causes degeneration of the retina and eventually resulting in total blindess.

SEBACEOUS ADENITIS: Degeneration of hair follicles causing hair loss and scaly skin.

VESTIBULAR DISORDER: Lack of co-ordination and loss of balance, but with no obvious sign of deformity in the ear.

All the above defects are inherited as simple autosomal recessives, such that the homozygous recessive state exhibits the problem but the homozygous dominant and heterozygous dominant (carrier) appear normal. Some defects are early in onset and can be identified in the young puppy but others are late in onset. For example, sebaceous adenitis may appear from 12 months onwards and PRA may not be seen until a dog is two years of age or more.

Increasingly, geneticists are looking at canine defects and trying to map them on the chromosomes but, as yet, very few are located. PRA has been isolated and located but only in the Irish Setter which has a slightly different version of the condition to the Akita. In the Irish Setter analysis of a blood or hair sample can identify dogs as PP (normal) Pp (carrier) or pp (affected) at a very early age and, thus, steps can be taken to eliminate Pp and pp animals from the breeding programme.

Since pp eventually leads to total irreversible blindness pp cases may be euthanised, but a Pp animal will lead a normal life though it would be unwise to use in a breeding programme. Sooner or later, PRA in the Akita and other breeds will be isolated and mapped and similar steps can then be taken as with Irish Setters. Other genes will also be identified and dealt with in similar fashion but, in the interim, breeders have to work on progeny and pedigree data to identify carrier animals.

When we are dealing with autosomal recessive traits it is important to realise that when an affected animal appears in a mating both parents must be carriers of the type Pp or Ll and that blame cannot be laid at the sire alone.

POLYGENIC TRAITS
Some defects are not inherited in this simple fashion but are complex in their mode of inheritance. Some traits such

as patellar luxation (dislocation of the kneecap, largely as a result of faulty construction) or hip dysplasia, are controlled in a much more complex fashion. They are known as polygenic traits which are controlled by many genes which may act in dominant and recessive ways but for which the numbers of genes involved is unknown. Traits of this kind often appear to show extreme variation and range like a normal curve with few animals at the extreme and most around the middle.

HIP DYSPLASIA

Hip dysplasia (HD) is a case in point. Dogs are born with unformed hip joints and with growth the acetabulum of the pelvis (socket) and the head of the thigh (femoral head) fit together tightly. In some dogs, the joint is slack and the hip does not fit tightly causing a kind of dislocation, and there can be a serious effect upon both pain and movement. Some dogs have such poor hip status that they need major surgery or hip replacement therapy or they are euthanised.

In most developed countries schemes exist to combat HD based upon radiographs of the hip taken at 12 months of age or more, and in which the radiographs are assessed by a panel of expert veterinarians and graded or scored. In the FCI countries, dogs are graded A,B,C,D or E with the best grade being A and the worst E. Sometimes the grades are divided into two by use of numbers so that one has a grade A1, A2 through to E1 and E2 giving 10 grades in total. In USA hip assessment by the Orthopaedic Foundation for Animals (OFA) is done at 24 months and dogs are graded as Excellent, Good, Fair, Borderline, Mild, Medium and Severe. Breeders seek to get into the first three grades and those in the last three are not published and do not get an OFA number. In Britain, hips are scored looking at 9 features of the hip which are each scored from 0 to 6 with lower numbers being best. One feature is scored 0-5 so that a dogs can score from 0 to 53 on each hip or 0 to 106 on both hips combined. Table 1 shows the distribution of Akita scores in Britain based on dogs scored up to October 1998.

Table 1
Distribution of scores in Akitas

Score Range	Number of Dogs	Percentage cumulative
0-5	322	26.1
6-10	483	65,3
11-20	298	89.5
21-30	70	95.2
31-40	29	97.6
41-50	10	98.4
51+	20	100.0

The mean score for the breed is 10.96 based on 1232 animals, which puts the breed well down the list in terms of breeds with substantial numbers scored. Two-thirds of the breed score 10 or less and only 5% are above 30 which means that in the UK the breed is in a fairly healthy state in hip terms.

However, some 30 dogs have scored in excess of 40 and the worst score located is 92. Table 2 shows the data by year of birth pooling into two-year periods.

There is no real evidence of change over this period of time, but there is some suggestion that scored numbers are declining though the most recent period.

WITHER HEIGHT
Thus far, we have looked at anomalies and defects but in truth the breeder is not concerned with these so much as with conformation, working ability and character. Clearly, no breeder wants anomalies and will or should seek to avoid them but most breeding activity should be directed at advancing conformation and character.

Most traits in the dog, e.g wither height, body length, shoulder angulation etc. will vary from one extreme to another. Thus male Akitas should, according to the Standard, range from 66-71 cms to the withers and will vary outside this range as well. The taller dogs will have more genes for 'tallness' than the dogs at the other extreme and in addition, unlike coat colour or traits like PRA, which are entirely genetic and unaffected by environment, height will be influenced,

Table 2
Akita scores by year of birth

Year born	No. of dogs scored	Score range	Mean score
<1984	36	0-37	10.66
1984-5	150	0-70	10.02
1986-7	242	0-70	11.99
1988-9	220	0-73	11.46
1990-1	158	0-66	11.25
1992-3	162	0-92	10.70
1994-5	177	0-55	9.76
1996-7	86	0-56	11.08

Litter size is not under the type of genetic control that can be selected for.

Photo: Keith Allison.

in part, by nutrition and environment so that the dog's height is a combination of genetic and environmental factors.

HERITABILITY

The degree to which a trait is inherited is termed its heritability, and the higher the heritability the easier it would be to select for that trait. Heritabilities can range from 0 to 100% but, in reality, range from around 10 to say 70%. Although no scientific data exist in the Akita, wither height in another similar sized breed is 65% heritable and body length about 44%. In contrast, litter size would be about 10-15%. Similarly hip dysplasia is between 25 and 55%

heritable depending upon the breed.

This means that if we bred only from those Akitas that came from very large litters (say over 12), the progress would be slow because the size of the litter is not under the type of genetic control that can be selected for. Attempts to increase litter size would be slow, and it might be easier to increase litter size by making a breed larger. However, attempts to select for taller dogs would be very effective because wither height is very highly inherited. By the same token, fear is a trait that is some 50% heritable and, thus, breeding from nervous or fearful animals would quickly lead to poorer characters within a breed.

BREEDING TO THE STANDARD

Of course, breeders are not always seeking to move a breed towards one or other extreme. Most breeders would seek to breed wither heights within the Standard and not exceed it, so they might not breed from the tallest dogs. Or if they did do so, because of other virtues, they might mate tall dogs to bitches well inside the Standard range. A breeder thus has to decide on priorities, and select to remain in the middle (as per height) or to move towards one extreme (as per better and better hips), or to rectify defects that have crept into the line.

Thus, a breeder with dogs that are getting longer than the 10:9 proportions expected in an Akita male would need to select to reduce body length, while a breeder whose dogs are too short will need to increase length. It follows that breeding not only involves some understanding of the genetics of traits but considerable appreciation of the Standard and of the assessment of dogs. A breeder who imagines that his stock are all perfect is unlikely to advance because of the inability to critically assess his stock, and a breeder who cannot tell a good dog from a bad one is likely to advance only by fortuitous accident.

There is no short-cut to knowledge and experience, but a true appreciation of the Standard of the breed, and of the faults and virtues of given dogs, is crucial to any breeding programme. Little is gained by trying to improve traits that are not under genetic control but which are the result of environment. A dog that excels in a trait because it was better fed or better managed is not

Selecting breeding stock is the hardest task a breeder must face.

Photo: Keith Allison.

necessarily better than one that was not so advantaged, even though the former may appear better. A bitch that produced a litter of 12 will be likely to produce a large litter next time because the repeatability of litter size is quite high, but her daughters may not produce litters like her, and may be no more prolific than the daughters of a bitch producing a litter size of six.

CHOOSING BREEDING STOCK

Deciding which dogs to breed from is the hardest task for the breeder. The more traits he wants to consider, the harder it will be to find any animal that measures up to all of them. One must select for heritable traits that are truly important and give less emphasis to minor features. A missing tooth or a light eye may be important, but not as crucial as major conformational or character traits. Breeders should not get hung-up on minor issues and ignore major ones. They should be selecting those animals that excel in the most traits that they are considering, but they might occasionally have to use an animal that is outstanding in some traits but fails in one or two. Provided that the trait in which the dog fails is not a highly important one, e.g. that it actually has PRA or is chronically dysplastic, it may be necessary to use the animal sparingly in order to obtain the virtues that it has.

Breeders seek to pick the best animals to breed from, and the extent to which they succeed will depend upon two major factors. Firstly, how good are the animals bred from relative to the mean of the population from which they came, and, secondly, how heritable is the trait. The greater the superiority of the breeding group and the higher the heritability, the greater the potential progress.

Some animals that are exceptional as specimens may not breed as well as they look because animal performance is not an exact guide. The higher the heritability the easier it is to predict performance, but, even with moderately high heritabilities, some dogs will breed worse or better than expected. Breeders have to consider progeny, because progeny tell a breeder what a sire(or dam) is producing, whereas actual merit of a dog simply tells one what it might do. When progeny become available in sufficient numbers, they will supercede the information gleaned on the dog itself. If the progeny are poor, that counts against continued use of an animal, and this is true even if the dog was outstanding. This is even more true of pedigree. Many breeders lay great stress on pedigree, but rarely is the pedigree as useful as the information on the dog itself – and a handful of progeny would be more useful than the pedigree.

12 *THE AKITA IN AMERICA*

As we have previously mentioned, the original importers of the Akita into America were mainly servicemen pet owners bringing their companions back home after the Second World War. It was these same people, mainly novices with little or no knowledge of breeding, or of the dog scene, who tried to form the first breed clubs, unfortunately without much success.

Eventually, the Akita Dog Association of America was formed in Southern California in 1952 but this had a closed membership. Not until 1956 was a second club formed, originally named the Akita Kennel Club. Three years later, in 1959, the word kennel was removed and in August 1960, registrations were filed and the Akita Club of America was born.

However, there were still conflicts and clashes of personalities and in 1963 a splinter group formed yet another club, which was named the American Akita Breeders. This club was quite successful with its show organisation and memberships. Unfortunately, there was a less than happy relationship between the two clubs. Several attempts were made to unite them. It took until 1969 to finally make the breakthrough, and the merger took place, naming the Akita Club of America as the official club.

Eventually, after much hard work, there was a meeting between the American Kennel Club (AKC) and the Akita Club of America, the outcome of which was that on October 24th 1972 the Akita was admitted to registry in the AKC Stud Books. From first being shown in the miscellaneous classes in 1955, it was seventeen years before the Akita was finally registered with the AKC; and from April 4th 1973, they were eligible to compete in the show ring for Championship status.

Am. Can. Mex. CACIB Ch. Gin-Gin Haiyaku-Go Of Sakusaku ROM, alias 'Chester', winning one of his many Working Groups.

Photo: Dick Alverson.

Am. Ch. HOTS Melvin O: A representative of the famous HOTS kennel recognised in many British pedigrees.

EARLY INFLUENCES

As these early dogs had not been chosen for their breeding, but were merely pets and companions, the original breeding programmes were very haphazard, with little regard to type or quality. Indeed, many of these first dogs were, in actual fact, rejects or of very poor type, which the Japanese were more than happy to off-load. It was not until the early 1970s, when more thought and planning went into the establishment of some of the early kennels, that names began to spring to the fore as recognised stud dogs and brood bitches. It was at this time that some of the famous kennels were formed that were to be with us for years and, indeed, in some cases, to this day.

Mr and Mrs D.D. Confer and Karen Keene imported the famous Grand Champions, Haru Hime, and the brindle, Teddybear of Toyohashi Seiko, whose names Akita enthusiasts all over the world will recognise. When mated, these two produced the famous litter containing Ch. Sakusaku's Tom Cat Go ROM, Sakusaku's Tiger Lily and Tusko's Star, who all went on to become top producers. Best remembered is the dog, sired by Tom Cat – American,

Am. Ch. Don-D's Dietka Of The HOT: Winning veteran bitch, aged 10 1/2 years, at the 1982 National Specialty. She also won the Brood Bitch class, the same day, with daughters aged seven years and eight months.

Touch Of Class Of Littlecreek (Am. Ch. Krugs Red Kadillac – Krugs Dame Na Nagagutsa) aged five months. Interestingly, one of the first litters born in England was from the famous Krugs kennel, owned by Bettye Krug who also played a large part in early American breedings.

Am. Ch. Okii Yubi's Mr Judge from the late Bob Campbell's famous kennel.

Canadian, Mexican, CACIB Champion Gin-Gin Haiyaku-Go of Sakusaku ROM, alias Chester. Originally owned by Joan Linderman, Chester was then sold to the New York kennel of Stephanie Rubenfeld, House of Treasures (HOTS), and Sara Kletter. The HOTS kennel is a name many British breeders will recognise from their early pedigrees.

During his show career, Chester was mainly handled by Fran Wasserman of the Date Tensha kennels, notching up over 200 Best of Breeds and 50 Group placements, which was some achievement at a time when Akitas were barely recognised. For those of us who have been lucky enough to watch Fran handle, we can understand how these two became a winning combination.

Another to make an early mark was the East coast kennel of Bettye and Francis Krug, which, again, will be recognised in early British pedigrees. Probably one of the most memorable was Krug's Santo, who became a dominant sire behind many eastern lines, including the Sakura kennels of Robert and Barbara Miller. The Millers bred their bitch Michiko of Kensha to Santo, producing Sakura's Chujitsu, who was to become the foundation bitch of Robert Campbell's highly successful Okii Yubi kennel.

Again, a recognisable name would be

the Akita Tani's kennel owned by Liz Harrell, whose dogs influenced many breedings on the West Coast. Walter and Camille Kam imported some of the early dogs from Japan, establishing their highly successful Triple K kennel. One of their outstanding males was the brindle Triple K Shoyu-Go.

Interestingly, when Akitas received Championship status in the USA in 1973, three of the first recorded Champions were owned by some of the aforementioned breeders. In this same year, a Group win was awarded to an Akita for the first time: Ch. Mitsu-Kuma-s Tora Oji-Go made history for the breed in Atlanta in October 1973; but it was not until 1976 that the breed saw its first Best in Show Akita in Ch. Wanchan's Akagumo.

In October 1976, the Akita Club of America held its first National Specialty show, hosted by the Akita Club of Greater Los Angeles. 104 Akitas competed in the regular classes and 36

in the sweepstakes. Mr C.L. Savage awarded Best in Sweepstakes to Gaylee's Fonzi No Kosetsu, co-owned and handled by Carol Foti, still one of today's top handlers in the breed. J. Council Parker judged the regular classes, awarding a memorable Best in Show to Ch. Gaylee's Okaminaga, owned and handled by Leon Nogue. Best of Opposite Sex went to Ch. Akita Tani's Kori Of Kosho-Ki, owned by Everett and Marlene Sutton, from whom the original imports to Kath and Gerald Mitchell's Kiskas kennel in the UK came. Winners Dog and Best of Winners was King's Nu Koya Kabuki Nisei and Winners Bitch, Takara's Miyuki.

DEVELOPMENT OF THE BREED

Over the next few years, Akitas enjoyed considerable success in the show ring and some of the record-breaking names came to the fore.

The year 1978 saw the arrival of

Am. Ch. Okii Yubi's Sachmo Of Makoto, owned by Bill and B.J. Andrews, bred by Bob Campbell. The most dominant sire in American breed history, also he appears in most top British pedigrees.

Am. Ch. The Real McCoy O'BJ. Imported by David in 1984, he was the only Sachmo son to come to England, and was also the sire of the famous 'Widow-Maker'.

Am. Ch. The Widow-Maker O'BJ (Am. Ch. The Real McCoy O'BJ – Am. Ch. The Same Dame O'BJ), owned and bred by Bill and B.J. Andrews. An outstanding show dog, he was the No. 2 sire all-time.

Am. Ch. O'BJ Kings Ransom (Am. Ch. The Widow-Maker OBJ – Am. Ch. The Mad Hatter O'BJ), owned by Lewis and Julie Hoehn.

Am. Ch. Goshens Chariots O'Fire. Owned by Lew and Julie Hoehn. He was sired by Am. Ch. O'BJ Kings Ransom out of Am. Ch. The Dame's On Target O'BJ.

Ch. Am. Ch. Goshens Heir Apparent At Redwitch (aged 17 months) en route to BIS and to becoming America's No. 1 Akita. He joined the Redwitch kennel at two years old.
Photo: Michele Perlmutter.

Ch. Tobe's Peking Jumbo, which also established what was to become the very famous Tobe kennel of Tom and Bev Bonnadonna, later renowned for producing some of the most outstanding heads. In 1979, a bitch led the rankings. Ch.Tamarlane's Silver Star was bred by Dr Sophia Kaluzniacki, who later bred what was to become the first British Champion, Ch. Tamarlanes, Veni Vidi Vici. Also in the rankings was Ch. Okii Yubi's Sachmo of Makoto, bred by Bob Campbell and owned by Bill and B.J. Andrews, but it was as a sire that Sachmo took the headlines, becoming the top producing Akita sire all-time and turning heads in the breed by finishing as the Number 1 Working Sire.

The O'BJ kennel of Bill and B.J. Andrews was to go on to become one of the leading kennels of the 1980s, not only producing a string of important winners, but also owning and/or breeding the top three Akita sires all-time, and some of the top producing dams.

Coming to the fore in the early 1990s was the Goshen kennel of Lew and Julie Hoehn which was destined to play its part in the foundation of our own Redwitch kennel. Three very dominant stud dogs came from this kennel, Am. Ch. O'BJs Kings Ransom, followed by his two sons, Eng. Am. Ch. Goshens Heir Apparent at Redwitch, who was later to dominate the British show scene, and Am. Ch. Goshens Chariots O'Fire.

It is impossible to mention all the leading kennels who have played a major part in the development of the Akita in this vast country, all producing their own lines and type. The breed has had its ups and downs, but America is blessed with some very clever and dedicated breeders who will always be the backbone of the Akita.

TRANSATLANTIC EXCITEMENT
While some of us in the UK had owned the breed for a short time and had read everything we could lay our hands on that was available on the breed, it was

Stud Dog Class at the 1985 National Specialty in Florida: Am. Ch. Jakuras Pharfossa Michael, Am. Ch. Pharfossa's Cujo (later imported to the UK by Jenny) and Am. Ch. Fu-Ki's Hideki Tojo.

Photo: Earl Graham.

Top right: Am. Can. Ch. Soho's Black Star, bred by Bill Wynn.

Photo: Ashbey.

Left: June Wynn with Am. Can. Ch. Bighorn's Last Ray Gin Bull, owned and bred by the Wynns.

Right: Am. Ch. Bighorn's Lord Of The Changsi winning Best in Sweepstakes at the National Specialty 1992.

Left: Am. Ch. Daijobu's Sherman.
Photo: Meyer.

Am. Ch. Daijobu's Vampirella taking BOB and Group at the Colorado KC.

in January 1985 that we finally got to see the Akita in numbers, when an excited band of owners, would-be owners or just plain enthusiasts made the trip to Florida to the Akita National Specialty.

Seeing the depth of quality and the type in numbers left a tremendous impression on us. At this time the Akita, for both of us, was our second breed, but the impact made by this visit sowed the seeds for what was to become a lasting challenge between us and the Akita.

Help and advice was freely given from people we had only read about and to this day many of these remain great friends and are still passing on their knowledge and sharing experiences.

Many, many Akitas left an impression on us, too many to mention, but there were those that stood out in our memory. Meeting Bill and B.J. Andrews for the first time, from whom David had already purchased The Real McCoy O'BJ, led to the opportunity to handle

and exercise O'BJ Bigson of Sachmo, who was not only one of the top winners, but is still today ranked the No. 3 sire overall. Also with them was a sixteen-week-old puppy, sired by McCoy, which everyone wanted to play with and admire. Who would have thought that this bundle of fun was later to become one of the top winners all-time and finish No. 2 sire in breed history. Although we were destined never to see him as an adult in the flesh, Ch. The Widow Maker O'BJ left a standard with us for the future that will never be forgotten.

Another memorable experience was that of seeing the beautiful white bitch Ch. Cotton Ginny O'BJ, handled by the extrovert Sid Lamont. This stunning bitch, with her striking black pigment, took Best of Breed over the males on more than one occasion during the Florida circuit. Other names which spring to mind are Ch. HOT's Mo's Barnaby Jones, owned by John D'Allessio and handled by Cathy Mines, who took Best of Breed at the National, Ch. Abbadon of Dune, Ch. Pharfossa's Michael and, interestingly, Ch. Pharfossa's Cujo, which Jenny and ex-husband John went on to purchase. Cujo played his part by becoming quite successful in the show ring within the early days in the UK, but unfortunately was sterile, so never produced in England.

This was an unforgettable experience and was to become the first of many trips to America, both to the Nationals and the Florida circuit, and to friends and breeders through whom we have gained more and more knowledge.

THE BREED TODAY

During the years following this first visit, up until the early 1990s, the Akita in America has gone through highs and lows in its development. Popularity, as with any breed, attracts unscrupulous breeders, and puppy mills sprang up all over the USA. ARSA, the US equivelant of the UK organisation Akita Rescue has, at times, had its hands full dealing with the problems these people left behind. Also, more and more health problems occurred, as more and more

Am. Ch. Tobe's Return Of The Jedai taking BIS at the Akita National Specialty 1995, handled by Sue Capone, judge Anne Rodgers-Clarke.

indiscriminate breedings took place. This is not peculiar to the Akita; it happens in most breeds when a boom in popularity occurs.

With the loss of some of the early influential kennels, it has taken time for the up-and-coming breeders to make their mark. However, the breed clubs have gone from strength to strength, with strong representatives in almost every State. Anyone visiting the National Specialties will see at first hand the dedication and enthusiasm of all those involved in the national club. With visitors coming from almost every country in the world, this event has a more international air every year.

A beautifully arranged photo-shoot at the Akita National Specialty 1995. Note the smartness of the handlers, Fran Wasserman and Carol Foti, who are both 'old hands' having handled Akitas since the 1970s, and are still two of the best around.
Photo: Booth.

THE SHOW SCENE IN AMERICA

Although smaller in numbers of dogs than the average Championship show in the UK, the glamour and razzmatazz of the American show scene has an appeal all of its own. It is the world of the professional handler, the motor-home and trailer and the "high-roller." Although entry fees may not vary much from those in the UK, it is difficult for the average British exhibitor to visualise the difference living in this vast country makes to the cost of keeping a dog on the show circuit. With most shows between one and three days away, the need to be self-sufficient is a must, with many handlers living in either large vans and trailers or motor-homes.

Probably the first obvious difference one encounters is the lack of benching at the shows, with dogs either being crated or kept in exercise pens at the trailers. All rings are wicker-fenced and have one entrance and exit, through which exhibitors pass to have their numbers checked on entering the ring. All major shows have Championship show status and entries vary tremendously from only two or three Akitas to fifty to sixty, depending on judges and areas, and up to four or five hundred Akitas at the National Specialty. The regional Specialties, which are hosted by smaller local clubs, also attract good entries.

THE POINTS SYSTEM

The award system in the USA is totally different from that which is used in the UK and dogs need to accumulate fifteen points to become Champions. Of these fifteen points, two awards need to be majors, which vary from three to five points depending on the number of dogs in competition. The remaining points may be accumulated in single increments if entries are small, but, a top-quality dog can fly to his title with three five-point majors if the owner or handler can find them.

CLASSIFICATION

Again different from the British classification, the American schedule shows classes for Puppy, Bred by Exhibitor, American-Bred and an Open class in each sex. It is from these classes that the points are won towards a title, without having to compete against Champions.

Best of Breed competition follows these regular classes and consists of all Champions, both dogs and bitches, plus Winners Dog and Winners Bitch, who are both eligible to compete for Best of Breed. Final awards are Best of Breed, Best of Winners and Best of Opposite Sex.

JUDGING

The schedule for each show gives a starting time for each breed and judges are expected to adhere to this, which means finishing by a given time also. Group judging is basically the same as seen in the UK now, with four group placements, but unlike in Britain, the Akita in the USA is seen in the Working Group.

HANDLING
Without doubt, the handling in the USA, whether it be by professional handlers or owner-handlers is, overall, far superior to that in Britain, with exhibitors smartly dressed and the presentation and showmanship of the dogs second to none. It can be seen at its best in Group competition.

THE RE-OPENING OF THE STUD BOOK
With the re-opening of the stud book in 1992, registrations were accepted for imports from Japan for the first time since 1974 causing great divergence of opinion both in and out of the show ring. One of the most successful kennels to emerge at this time, introducing Japanese imports and cross-breeding the pure Japanese and American type, was the Northlands kennel of Loren and Christina Egland, to whom we have turned for an up-to-date and concise record from 1992 to the present day.

IMPORTS AND OUTCROSSES IN THE USA 1992 TO 1998
by Loren Egland

One of the most important events in the history of the Akita in the United States was the AKC's recognition of the breed on April 4th 1973. The most significant event that affected the direction the Akita breed would take happened on February 28th 1974. At that time, the stud book was closed to further registration of Akitas as foundation stock in the United States. Only 139 pedigrees from this foundation were ever used for breeding. This was the gene pool on which the Akita breed in the US was based.

The only event that may equal, or even surpass, the significance of the 1974 stud book closing was the April 13th 1992 news release by the AKC. It stated that during their April meeting, the board of directors of the AKC approved the addition of the Japan Kennel Club to the AKC's primary list of foreign dog registry organizations. This action permitted dogs registered with the JKC imported into the United States to be eligible for AKC registration. This made it possible again to import Akitas from the country of origin and add them to the gene pool of Akitas in the United States.

How this event would effect the Akita in the United States was a hot topic among Akita fanciers. Some felt this was a godsend, while others were vehemently opposed to it. However, the deed was done and speculation of what would happen appeared to be on everyone's mind.

Many were concerned that the Japanese imports did not meet the AKC Akita Standard. Some common objections included the observation that

Northland's Shades Of Sunset, aged ten weeks (3/4 import lines). Owned by Loren and Christina Egland.

Northland's Shades Of Sunset: Aged eight months. Baltimore Akita Club Best in Match over 37 Akitas. Best of Winners and BOS at the Akita Club's supported entry. Handled by Carol Foti.

most American-bred Akitas were larger, with more bone and heavier muzzles than the general population of Akitas in Japan. Many felt this difference was because the JKC Akita Standard was so different. However, the JKC and AKC Akita Standards are very similar, except for the JKC's restrictions on colour and markings. Though the JKC Standard colours and markings fit well within the AKC Standard, the reverse is not always true. So often, when Akita fanciers were speaking of differences in the written Standards, they were actually speaking about the differences in the general type of the Akitas from Japan compared to the general type of Akitas in the United States.

Another issue that worries some is that of health. It has not been a common practice of Japanese breeders to check hips or eyes for problems as is regularly practised in the United States. Many wonder if Akitas imported from Japan will bring with them genetic problems. Others believe that out-crossing to a new gene pool would result in better genetic health. Would the Japanese imports be as healthy, less healthy or more healthy than the Akitas in the United States? It has now been six years since the reopening of the stud books to imported Akitas. It appears that the health and temperaments of the imported Akitas are no worse than the American stock. Perhaps dog genetics work the same in other parts of the world as it does in America. It should be noted that the JKC has started to address health issues. Unfortunately, no-one really knows all the genetic health problems that could be present in their stock, no matter what country they are from.

OUT-CROSSING
Perhaps the main issue that excites some and horrifies others is the out-crossing

of Japanese imports and domestic Akitas! Would such breedings improve the Akita, or would it result in less overall quality? Would a new breed be the result? This prospect has been viewed by some as very undesirable, thinking that it would add to the confusion of breeders and judges. On the other hand, is this view a realistic one? Would these out-crosses destroy the exotic beauty of the imports?

Would the type of Akita many Americans fell in love with be ruined? How many generations would it take to realize the potential benefits or repercussions from out-crossing such extremes in type to each other? Would breeders care enough to choose quality animals for breeding? Should breeders play it safe by not out-crossing their American Akitas to the Japanese imports because they would have a better chance of producing more AKC Champions per litter instead of maybe only producing one Champion in an out-crossed litter? Should breeders make the sacrifice of producing fewer Champions in the first out-crossed litter while looking down the road for the potential Champions of higher quality in the second or third generation? The JKC Honorary Chairman, Mr Kariyabu, suggested that once an out-cross of this nature was done, it would take twelve to fifteen years and five generations to realize the completion of a breeder's efforts. How many breeders would be able to follow through with such a commitment? These were some of the questions that would be likely to be answered with time.

THE SHOW SCENE
There are some breeders who prefer to separate dog evaluation and dog breeding from what happens in the show ring. They only trust their own eye for a dog. For those who fall into this category there are photographs, accompanying this discussion, of Japanese imports and the offspring from various out-crosses of these imports with American stock, for self-evaluation. For the show exhibiting enthusiast, a brief overview of some of the highlights in the AKC conformation ring and the Los Angeles Akita Inu Hozonkai (AKIHO) Branch in the United States will be presented from the opening of the import registration in 1992 until the date of winning (1998).

Rei: Aged five years. A full import from Japan – a Meiyosho winner in Japan, Owned by Loren and Christina Egland.

The first Akita to be imported from Japan to the USA in 1992 was a five-year-old red bitch named Hachihime of Onishi Kensha. She was bred by Kiyomi Onishi and was imported by Mr Frank Sakayeda. She was first shown in the open class at the 1992 ACA National Specialty held in Houston, Texas on Saturday, November 14th 1992, where she was awarded Winners Bitch for a 5 point major. As evidenced by the loud cheering, this import bitch was a crowd favourite, as she had good bone and full body with an exquisite headpiece. Although she had whelped puppies in Japan, she never produced puppies in America. This was very disappointing.

In September of 1992, Mr Frank Sakayeda imported a two-month-old red bitch for us. Frank and Alice Sakayeda remained as co-owners. Her name was Tsubakihime of Kyushu Fukabori and her call name was simply Japan. She was bred by Ukiyoshi Fukabori Kasugashi. Her sire was Kita No Unryu of Sasahara Kensha CD and her dam was Yoshi No Hana of Kyushu Fukabori. Japan was awarded Best in Match at the Golden Gate Akita Club Specialty match. A short time later she won Best Opposite Sex in Sweepstakes at the Regional Specialty. She was only shown seven or eight times in the AKC ring until she was four years old, but did pick up four points and a couple of Reserves at these shows.

Japan was maturing nicely and at the age of four, she was seriously shown, taking points on six of the eight weekends she was shown, to become only the second import bitch to achieve her AKC Championship. In February 1996 Japan became the first, and still the only, bitch ever to receive the Gold Award at the Los Angeles Branch AKIHO show. The judge was Mr Toshio Kashiwabara from Matsuyama, Japan. His dedication to the quality of Akitas was recognised when he was appointed as an Assistant Department Director of Judges in June 1993. His residency in the department started in December 1972.

Shortly after Frank Sakayeda imported Japan, he also imported Japan's sire Kita No Unryu of Sasahara Kensha. Ryu was his call name and he obtained a Companion Dog obedience title at the end of his name. Ryu's sire is Ise Unryu of Ise Meiwas Kensha, a very famous dog in Japan, who was reportedly sold for over $150,000.00. Frank was able to obtain Ryu at about two years of age, partly because his red colour was a lighter shade than the ideal.

Around the same time as Frank Sakayeda imported Ryu, he also brought back from Japan a red male puppy who was sired by Ryu. His name was Tetsuryu of Takeshita Kensha. His call name was Sho and he was owned by Bill Bobrow, Carol Parker, Camille Kam and Frank Sakayeda. Sho was the first male import to become an AKC

145

Champion and he also obtained a CDX title. He was the No. 1 Obedience Akita in 1994, 1995 and 1997 and was the first Akita to compete in the Gaines Cycle Dog Obedience Championships. Sho was also in a movie, playing the part of O.J.Simpson's Akita, Kato.

Another Akita of note was also brought to the USA by Frank Sakayeda for Ben and Melanie Herrera. He was a silver and black brindle male puppy named Tetsumine of Takeshita Kensha, with the call name Tora. Tora became the first male Akita to win the Gold Award at the 1996 Los Angeles Branch AKIHO show. The Herreras recently became owners of another brindle male, imported and co-owned by Frank Sakayeda. He is an older dog named Daietsu-Go and he won the Meiyosho Award at the AKIHO Headquarters show in Japan.

Mrs Pat Szymanski has imported about a dozen Akitas from Japan. One of these was a five-year-old Meiyosho winning red bitch, named Matsumi. Matsumi took Best of Breed over eight Champions and a Working Group 1st, becoming the first imported Akita to finish her AKC Championship. Matsumi's daughter Bara is the first full import breeding in America to finish her AKC Championship and she did so on April 5th 1998. Matsumi's son Musha was also close to finishing and had both his majors.

Pat also imported another Meiyosho winning bitch. Her name is Rei. She is a lovely brindle and won a five point major at the only AKC show in which she was entered.

One of Pat Szymanski's most recent imports is a red, six-year-old male, named Tai Zan. He was a double Akiho Gold Award winner in Japan; however, Tai Zan won the only Gold Award at the February 1998 Los Angeles Branch AKIHO show, so he is now a Triple Gold winner.

Kobun's Taisho-Go is a red male

owned by Ben Herrera and Kiyoski Yamazaki. Taisho's sire was a deep red import named Shinto. Taisho's dam was an import named Tenkohime. Taisho is AKC and AKIHO registered. At both the 1995 and the 1996 LA Branch AKIHO show, Taisho won the judges' award for Best Male in Show. Then in 1997, Taisho won the Gold Award. Only Akitas entered in the Seiken (over thirty months) class can compete for the Gold, Silver and Bronze Awards.

An eleven-month-old brindle male named Northland's Out of the Shadows was presented the judges' award for Best Male in Show at the 1998 LA AKIHO show. His call name is Shadow. Shadow's sire was 1996 Gold Winner Tora and his dam was the 1996 Gold Winner and AKC Champion, Japan. When Japan was bred to Tora and produced Shadow, it was the first time she had been bred to an import stud. The 1998 AKIHO judge was Mr Hiroyuki Yumashita who has participated in both regional and national shows in Japan since 1977. His dedication to the quality of Akita dogs was recognised when he was appointed the Department Director of Judges in June 1997.

OUTCROSSES IN CONFORMATION

This brings us to the next part of this discussion. How have the outcrosses of American-bred Akitas to Japanese-bred Akitas fared in the AKC conformation

Meisei's She's The One: A 7/8th import, aged three months.

ring? First of all, to our knowledge, there have been only three Japanese import bitches bred to American-bred males. One of these bitches was leased to accomplish the breeding, and we are unaware of any points being awarded to the offspring of this mating. Another has very young puppies, born in late 1997. The other import bitch was Japan and she was bred to three different males of American or part-American breeding. The possible reason for so few import bitches being out-crossed to American studs is that the resulting puppies can only be registered by the AKC. If the import bitch owner breeds her to an import male, the resulting puppies can be dual-registered by AKC and AKIHO. So, usually, the outcrosses that have occurred are American-bred bitches to import studs.

Ch. Tsubakihime Of Kyushu Fukabori: Japanese import, aged four years. The only import bitch to win the LA Branch Akiho Gold Award. One of two import bitches to become an AKC Champion. Owned by Loren and Christina Egland.

Another point of interest is that only two AKC Champion titled bitches have had litters from an import stud, as of April 1998. The first one was Ch. Frakari Starfire O'Northland, who was brindle with white markings. The other was Ch. Kobun's Sanko, who had a litter by the import Shinto, then later completed her Championship and was then bred to the import Tora. Owners of Champion bitches no doubt believe that breeding to an AKC Champion stud will make the resulting puppies more desirable or valuable.

Let us begin with Japan's outcrossed offspring. When she was bred to the large white Northland's Snow Panther, she produced an AKC major-pointed bitch who became a Canadian Champion. Her name is Can. Ch. Northland's Aka Kitsu of SDM, and she is owned by Suzette Morettini and Bev Wilkinson. A litter brother named Northland's On the Prowl was ten months old when he won Best in Match at the Golden Gate Akita Club Specialty Match over 32 Akita. Prowler, as he was called, also was Best in Sweepstakes at a regional Akita Specialty and was nearly finished when he went to live with some folks who did not continue to show him.

Japan's next litter was out of Ch. T'stones The Hustler. This was his first litter. A bitch was produced named Northland's Embers at Dawn. Her call name was Ember. When she was almost nine months old, she attended the 1995

National Akita Specialty in Chicago. There she won second in her Sweepstakes class, first in her futurity class and first in the regular six-to-nine month class over an entry of twelve bitches. Ember was Best Opposite Sex at a GGAC Supported Entry and on April 11th 1998, she won Winners Bitch for a major at the Channel Islands Akita Club First Independent Regional Specialty. On May 25th 1998, Ember finished her Championship at San Fernando KC.

Japan's third litter was out of her half-brother, American and Canadian Ch. Northland's Shere Khan of SDM. Since Shere Khan is one-half import breeding, the resulting puppies were three-quarter import lines. A white-faced, red male was produced named Ch. Northland's King Of Beasts, or Lion for short. When Lion was eight months old, at his second show he won Best of Breed over several top Champions for a four-point major and then placed third in the Working Group, all breeder-owner-handled by me. At fourteen months, he won Reserve Winners Dog to a five-point major from the Bred by Exhibitor class at the IEAC Regional Specialty. Lion was allowed to mature, and at 28 inches tall, he has turned out to be one of the largest dogs in the Akita ring, which is quite unexpected considering he is 75% import breeding. He has just turned two years old and won Winners Dog for a five-point major and an Award of Merit over Champions at the

Northland's King Of Beasts: Aged 14 months (3/4 import breeding). Group placer and multiple BOB over specials, Reserve Winners Dog Regional Akita Specialty, Winners Dog and Award of Merit at Regional Akita Specialty.

Las Vegas Akita Club regional Specialty on April 3rd 1998. On April 19th 1998, Lion finished his Championship with three majors.

Turning our attention to the American-bred bitches that have been bred to import studs, we will start with the AKC Ch. Frakari Starfire of Northland, aka Star. Star's first four breedings were to four different American studs, but none of these breedings resulted in a pregnancy. Finally, her fifth breeding was to the import Kita no Unryu of Sasahara Kensha CD. This produced only one pup, a white male who was named Ch. Northland's Snow Drift. He is owned by Barbara Hampton and co-owned with his breeders, the Eglands. His call name is Drifter and on April 5th 1998, he finished with four majors, including a Winners Dog and a Best of Winners at two Akita Club of Las Vegas Regional Specialty weekends.

Since only one puppy was produced, the Ryu x Star breeding was repeated. This time a litter of three was born, two white males and one brindle male. One of the white males was sold to a pet home and the other white male was sent to Frank Sakayeda as a stud fee puppy. His name was Northland's Shiro Tetsu Satori and he was called Tetsu. He is owned by Frank Sakayeda and Bill Bobrow. The brindle male became Am. Can. Ch. Northland's Shere Khan of

SDM, owned by Suzette Morettini, and Bev Wilkinson, and bred by the Eglands.

The litter brothers, Tetsu and Shere Khan, were both exhibited at the 1995 National Akita Specialty in the six-to-nine months puppy classes. Tetsu won Best Puppy in Sweepstakes over an entry of 64 Akitas. Litter brother, Shere Khan, won Best Puppy in Futurity as well and second in the regular six-to-nine month class with 13 entries. Already an American and Canadian Champion, Shere Khan's future looks bright at only three years of age. At the Regional Specialty weekend GGAC Supported Entry of 71 Akitas, including a dozen Champions, Shere Khan won the Award of Merit. During the Las Vegas Akita Club regional weekend, three weeks later on April 4th

GROUP FIRST
MID CONTINENT
KENNEL CLUB
1993
PHOTO BY PETRULIS©

Ch. Matsumi: A Group winning bitch. Owned by Pat Szymanski.

1998, Shere Khan won another Award of Merit.

Star's third and last litter was by the import, Tochimuso of Kurume Hirose, who was called Hank. He was owned by Hank Kapali and Frank Sakayeda. This litter only produced one puppy, a red, white-faced bitch. Her name is Northland's The Cats Meow. Owned by Cornelius Campbell and co-owned by the Eglands, Meow is very large, weighing 98 pounds. She finished her Championship on July 4th 1998 with a couple of Best of Breeds over top competition.

Meow was bred to an import named Mugenmaru Go Kurume Hirose, who was imported by Frank Sakayeda for Cornelius Campbell but is now owned by Taire Arndt. This breeding produced a three-quarter import bitch named Northland's Shades of Sunset. Called Shady, at her first show at eight months of age, she was Winners Bitch. In March 1998, Shady won Best in Match over an entry of 37 Akitas at the Baltimore Akita Club Specialty match. At Shady's second AKC show in April 1998, she won Best of Winners and Best of Opposite Sex over Champions for a five-point major at an Akita Club Supported Entry. Her dam, Meow, was Reserve Winners Bitch.

Meow's sire, Hank was also bred to a half-import bitch. This produced a Hawaiian three-quarter import Champion named Koa, owned by Diane and Andrew Sumera in Hawaii.

Alan and Tina Kuroda bred Taisho's brother, Kuroki's The Next Generation, to a large American bitch, Kuroki's Red Hot Fury, and produced a red bitch named Kuroki's Rhythm's Gonna Getcha. Rhythm is owned by Lauri Peifer and won the Best in Match at her first show at the ACIV Akita Specialty Match. At the 1996 National Specialty, Rhythm took second place in the nine-to-twelve month Sweepstakes class with an entry of 17 bitches. At the 1997 National Specialty, Rhythm won Best Opposite Sex to the Grand Maturity winner. She is over two years old and recently won a five-point major during the Regional Specialty weekend and now needs only a three-point major to finish her AKC Championship. Rhythm is also a United Kennel Club Champion and holds a UKC Agility title, an AKC Novice Agility title, CGC and is working toward an obedience and tracking title. Future plans are to breed Rhythm to Can. Am. Ch. Northland's Shere Khan of SDM.

Rhythm's breeders, the Kurodas, recently imported a Taisho (formerly called Meiyosho) winning brindle male and two red bitch puppies from Japan to add to the gene pool in the USA.

Carol Howton recently bred the brindle American bitch, Tetsu Hito's Kori Coca, to Aurora's Shinjitsu, who is a white male of import lines bred by Diane Smith, who has imported some Akitas from Japan. A brindle bitch puppy, born August 21st 1997, named

Pr & Am. Ch. Akasta's Akarui Bara: The first Akita Champion of 100 per cent import lines bred in America. Owned by Pat Szymanski.

Ichiban's Hachimisu-Go, already shows great promise.

The first and only seven-eighths import breeding was from a male of full import lines, named Aurora's Tenmeimaru-Go, bred with Lion's three-quarter import litter sister, Northland's Femme Fatale, owned by John Cortez and co-owned with the Eglands. Of the two puppies born on December 14th 1997, only one survived. Her name is Meisei's She's the One and at three months of age, she appears to have much to offer.

The foregoing report does not include every Akita imported from Japan or every breeding or show win. An endeavor was made to mention all Akitas and breedings of greatest interest and to present their most notable wins. Most of the progeny of these outcrosses

are still very young and immature, so it is likely these will have future successes at upcoming dog shows. Very few import-to-domestic breedings have taken place over the last six years. If the animals bred were of mediocre quality, or if care was not practiced in choosing Akitas that physically compensate each other, the results may have been so disappointing as to cause those breeders not to try such an outcross again. Many prefer to let others breed the first outcross generation so that they can eventually breed to the better Akitas produced from these outcrosses in order to preserve the oriental qualities found in the AKC Standard. These breeders only want part of the import lines to enhance their stock. A few take a different approach and want some size or bone or structure enhancement from the American stock and then try to hold those assets when breeding back to the import stock in the second generation, in order to maintain the Japanese type.

If it is a breeder's desire to produce a work of art that is a credit to the Standard and endowed with excellence in every detail, that breeder may be willing to spend the time needed to see the realization of that dream. This course would probabiy result in less AKC show success along the way. A breeder whose desire is to produce the greatest number of AKC Champions would be well-advised to only breed American stock to American stock and not incorporate import genes into the breeding program.

Probably what keeps most people from showing their import Akitas regularly, if at all, is the same reason many people do not obtain import stock to begin with, even though they may find some imports attractive. It is because they realize they are unlikely to win with imports. How is one import orange going to compare to, or compete with, twenty domestic apples? How would the best American-bred Akitas do at a JKC show, even if the colour and markings were compatible with the Japanese Standard? The American-bred Akita's type would not often win in Japan either.

SPLITTING THE BREED

Few breeders have made the effort to incorporate the imports into their breeding programmes over the last six years. However, now that there are some quality outcrosses carrying import genes that fit the AKC Standard well, they could be used for future breedings. It seems that the time is near when a split in the breed would be a reasonable solution, and for everyone to consider the benefits of this. Breeders who want to keep their options open to future use of recent import genes will still have that available to them in the outcrosses that have already been produced. The breeders who love and would prefer to continue breeding and exhibiting the Mastiff-type Akita found in America will not have to worry about the

occasional loss in the show ring as a result of a few judges who will reward a good-quality Japanese-type Akita. The breeders who share the vision of restoration to a Japanese type of dog can remain true to that effort and also win at the AKC shows on a regular basis, because an orange will no longer look out of place when compared to other oranges instead of a ring full of apples.

If the breed were to split, the American type and the Japanese type could be preserved, with both being represented in the Working Group. It is quite likely that several people would enjoy owning, breeding and exhibiting both breeds at the same time, especially when they could now win with both types.

What would be the best way to split the breed into two breeds? It has been suggested that it could be accomplished simply by a division based on colour and markings. However, that alone would not ensure a division of two separate and distinctive-looking breeds, since many American-type Akitas are Japanese Standard colour compatible, but they are not true Japanese type. Because the current import lines are so different from what has been bred in America since AKC recognition, it seems that a good percentage (at least 50% or more at this time, or 75% or more if separated later) of current import lines should be a requirement, along with Japanese colour and markings, in order to qualify for the Japanese-style Akita. All future breedings within this side of the split would be forced to breed these outcrosses to the true Japanese-type Akitas, thus preserving this type as a breed that is different than the American side of the breed split.

The same reasoning would hold true if 50% or more American lines were necessary for entrance into the American Akita. The 50% rule seems reasonable in both directions if the split was done now before more breedings took place. An exception to the 50% rule would be if a dog of more than 50% import lines did not meet the colour and marking standard of the JKC (such as a black mask): it must only be eligible for the American side. This should not be a major problem, since very few three-quarter import breedings have taken place and they usually have Japanese colour and markings. There are only one or two dogs of such breeding that do not fit the JKC colour standard.

Though there are three or four high-quality Akitas of 75% or more import lines that have attributes that could benefit the pure import stock without altering their true Japanese type, some feel that the only way to separate the breed would be to accept only 100% import lines since 1992 into the Japanese side. The reason for this opinion is easy to understand. It may be the only way to be sure the Japanese type is preserved. It is feared that most breeders do not fully understand the differences in type compared to outcrosses and to American stock with Japanese colour. This option for a split should also be considered.

The naming of the two breeds that result from an Akita breed split would be another issue that would need to be decided. Greater Asian Spitz or American Bear Dog are a couple of names that have been suggested for the American side. American Akita, North American Akita and Western Akita have also been mentioned as possible names. It is doubtful that a separation of the Akita breed in the United States would receive an affirmative vote of the Akita Club of America members if the name of the American side of the Akita breed split did not include the name Akita.

It is uncertain what the ramification will be for the Akita in America if the FCI divides the breed and names the new breed of American type something without the name Akita attached to it. Should the Akita Club of America be proactive or reactive? Will leaving this issue alone be in the best interest of the Akita in America? Should a breed split take place sooner, later or not at all? It seems everyone has an opinion on the subject. One thing is certain, there will be no lack of interest as future events unfold.

Loren Egland

13 THE AKITA IN BRITAIN

Akitas were introduced into the UK as early as 1937, although little was known about them as they came in as companions and pets. In the early forties a serviceman from Canada imported a white male. After serving his quarantine period this dog was passed on to the kennelmaid at the Quarantine Station, a Mrs Jenson, owing to a change in circumstances of his previous owner. It became apparent quite quickly that this Akita was very dominant with other dogs and there were a few early skirmishes. After coping on her own with him for some time, Mrs Jenson had to make the sad decision to have him put down when his temperament deteriorated at only four years of age.

Between the early 1940s and 1980 little more was heard about Akitas. Although several were imported, we have very little factual information as their owners, believing them to be a rare breed and, owning them solely as pets, thought they could not be registered with the Kennel Club.

And so it was not until 1980 that interest was stirred in the breed by the importing of Miss Marion Sargent's fawn and white bitch, Davos Watakyshi Tomo Dachi of Tegwani, or Tanya as she was known. Tanya was first shown in 1981 and did well in the Any Variety classes. Exhibited at Crufts in 1982, she took Best Opposite Sex, winning many admirers on the way.

Following hot on Tanya's heels was a black and white pinto female, imported from California by Gerald and Kath Mitchell, Kosho Ki's Kiki of Kiskas.

The import male, cared for by Mrs Jenson.

Davos Watakyshi Tomo Dachi Of Tegwani, imported by Marion Sargent in 1981.

The first Japanese-bred import, Yukihime Go Of Rediviva.

The first of the present-day imports direct from Japan then followed. Mrs Beryl Mason brought in a solid white female, Yukihime Go of Rediviva, who was first exhibited at the Ladies Kennel Association in 1982. In partnership with Mike and Joyce Window, Gerald and Kath Mitchell then imported

another dog, this time a male, Kosho Ki's Kai of Lindrick And Tegwani.

THE INFLUX OF IMPORTS
Great interest had now been generated and these early imports were swiftly followed by Akitas from many different areas of the USA.

Together with Sheila Gonzalez-Camino, Meg Purnell-Carpenter imported the first Akitas to come from the famous O'BJ kennel of Bill and B.J. Andrews, one male and two females. The male was to play a significant part in the early establishment of the breed in this country. O'BJ Aces High was bred to one of his accompanying females, Am. Ch. O'BJ Sachette No

Kosho-Ki's Kai Of Lindrick And Tegwani: One of the first imported males. Owned by Mike Window and Marion Sargent.

Am. Ch. Sachette No Okii Yubi: Imported by Meg Purnell-Carpenter, she produced some top-class show and foundation stock.

Okii Yubi, resulting in a litter of seven puppies. He was also bred to Tanya, the bitch imported by Marion Sargent, who produced seven puppies as well. Aces High was then exported to Australia.

In February 1983, another female was imported by Gerald and Kath, Kosho Ki's Kimono of Kiskas, and an adult male, Kosho Ki's Song for Adam O'TK at Teldale, was brought in by Malcolm and Ingrid Hamlet.

The Mitchells bred their first import bitch, Kiki, to Adam resulting in their first litter to carry the Kiskas affix. Adam proved his worth not only as a sire but also as a show dog, becoming the breed's first-ever Best of Breed winner at Eastwood Open Show.

During 1983, Frank and Brett Cassidy of the famous Littlecreek

Newfoundland and Skye Terriers, imported into their quarantine kennels two bitches in whelp. The first recorded litter born in the UK was to Youtoo's Sumico of Littlecreek born on July 21st 1983. This was quickly followed by Krug's Dame Na Nag Agusta who whelped on August 9th 1983.

Also into this quarantine kennel came two young males who were both to be very successful in the Akita's early days in the show ring and as sires. Frank and Brett retained ownership of Krug's Big Mac of Littlecreek, and the other, Arrowcreek's Redman of Fire, became the foundation dog of Helen and Pieter Burke's kennel.

During the next few years, many more imports followed, so widening the gene pool and establishing the foundation of many of today's leading kennels.

Kosho Ki's Song For Adam O'TK At Teldale. Owned by Mr and Mrs M. Hamlet.

Arrowcreek's Redman Of Fire: Imported by Frank and Brett Cassidy, and owned by Pieter and Helen Burke. After a successful show career, this dog went on to become the lead dog on Pieter's racing team.

THE FIRST BREED CLUBS

As interest in the Akita grew, so too did the need to have a club to represent and look after the welfare of the breed. With owners coming from a variety of different breeds and, indeed, from first-time dog owners, there was obviously a great divergence of opinion. In January 1983, the Japanese Akita Club of Great Britain was formed, but unfortunately events were to follow exactly the same pattern as those of the American clubs. A rift between its members caused a splinter group to branch off to form the Japanese Akita Society in February 1984.

After both clubs fought for recognition without success, the Kennel Club called for harmony within the breed, and eventually an open meeting was called for all interested parties, which led to the formation of the first officially recognised breed club, the Japanese Akita Association, in February 1987, and the disbanding of the Society. Although the formation of this club did not satisfy all parties, and the road ahead was to be a rocky one, it did pave a way for the breed which still remains strong today.

EARLY SHOW SUCCESSES

From August 1983, the show ring was buzzing with Akitas making their first impacts. Following successes in the Any Variety and Rare Breed classes, Akitas were allocated their own classes at the British Utility Breeds (BUBA)

Kiskas Triad from Gerald and Kath Mitchell's first litter by Kosho Ki's Song For Adam O'TK At Teldale out of Kosho Ki's Kiki Of Kiskas. Triad had a successful early show career.

Championship Show in December 1983. Best of Breed was Arrowcreek's Redman of Fire and more significantly, taking the headlines with Best Puppy in Show was Gerald and Kath's baby, Kimono.

Crufts 1984 saw seven Akitas exhibit in the Any Variety Not Separately Classified (AVNSC) section. These were all early imports. They created tremendous interest, not only with people in other breeds, but also with the general public. Many of the successes in 1984 were by puppies born in the first litters of 1983. Kiskas Triad, from the Mitchells' first litter won a round of the Spillers/Dog World Pup of the Year Competition, handled by one of the top professional handlers, Geoff Corrish.

David (Killilea), together with his ex-wife, had two successful puppies that year. Black Samari of Littlecreek, who is still the only solid brindle Akita to take Best of Breed at Championship level, and Overhills Marlows Miracle, who

Kiskas Yum Yum (Kosho's Ki's Song For Adam – Kosho Ki's Kimono At Kiskas): This bitch had a successful show career including winning BOS Crufts 1986. Owned by Brenda and Brian Pearson and Katherine Pearson-Smith.

went on to be one of Britain's most successful Akitas over the next few years.

What a difference a year can make! From seven Akitas in 1983, BUBA had forty entered in December 1984, where Best of Breed went to Mesdames Andrews, Brook and Ree's Touch of Class of Littlecreek.

Crufts 1985 saw David once again in the limelight. Nineteen Akitas were entered in AVNSC and it was Miracle's litter sister, Lizzies Girl, who stole the show by taking Best AVNSC and being the first Akita ever to appear in the Group ring at Crufts.

During the next two years registrations in the breed grew, and

Kosho Ki's Kimono Of Kiskas: Imported and owned by Gerald and Kath Mitchell. The breed's first Best Puppy In Show.

Photo: Dalton.

Kiskas Omen Of Hoffman (litter brother to Triad): First BOB Akita at Crufts, 1988. Owned by Joan and Dave Rushby.

Photo: Dave Freeman.

more and more Championship shows scheduled classes for Akitas. Voodoo Doll of Kiskas, owned by Gerald and Kath Mitchell became the first Akita ever to take a Group win at an all-breed Championship show, at Paignton in 1986, again handled by Geoff Corrish.

September 1986 saw the first junior warrant winner in the breed. Owned by Chris and Sue Thomas, Teldale Tabasco at Farmbrook was bred by Ingrid and Malcolm Hamlet.

In 1987, classes were scheduled at Crufts for the first time. There were twelve classes for Akitas with 81 dogs making 112 entries. Best bitch was Gordon and Irene Rattray's Northern Hope at Varenka, but in the spotlight was Kiskas Omen of Hoffman, winning Best of Breed for owners Joan and Dave Rushby. Both of these dogs were home-bred Akitas from imported stock.

From here on, the Akita went from

Kiskas Ty-Ffoon (Kiskas Bulletproof At Yorlander – Kosho Ki's Kimono At Kiskas) aged 8 1/2 years. Owned by Brenda and Brian Pearson and Katherine Pearson-Smith.

Left: Ch. Am. Ch. Tarmalanes Veni Vidi Veci handled by Rusty Short in the Group ring at Crufts 1990 after winning the first CC awarded to an Akita. He went on to become the first Akita Champion in Britain, and the first to win BIS All Breeds at a Championship show. Photo: Dalton.

success to success, growing in popularity to become one of the most admired new breeds in the Utility Group. At Crufts 1990, Challenge Certificates (CCs) were on offer for the breed for the first time. Dog CC and Best of Breed went to the American import Am. Ch. Tarmalanes Veni Vidi Vici, owned then by Mike Window and Marion Sargent and handled by top American professional handler Rusty Short, who had previously handled Victor to many of his top wins in America. Before returning to the USA, Victor went on to become the first British Champion and the first Akita ever to win Best in Show at an all-breeds Championship show. This was at the Welsh Kennel Club in August 1990.

EARLY INFLUENTIAL KENNELS
Three kennels sprang to the fore in the mid-eighties, all importing a selection of dogs from different parts of the USA, and each of them going on to play a large part in the development of the breed in the early years.

Gerald and Kath Mitchell's Kiskas kennel not only became one of the most dominant in the show ring at this time, but also produced some of the early litters born in this country, the progeny from which went on to become quite successful over the following years.

The Littlecreek kennel of Frank and Brett Cassidy produced the first litter to be born in quarantine in this country. They also imported some of the most

Ch. Brandeezi Quite-A-Gent At Stecal: The first British-bred Champion, winning his third CC under Ellis Hulme at the Welsh KC 1991.
Bred by Pauline and Eddie Hayes, owned by Carol Bevis and Steve Dutton.

161

consistently used early sires in Big Mac of Littlecreek and Arrowcreek's Redman of Fire. Although not so active in the show ring themselves, the Littlecreek kennel produced a great deal of foundation stock, as well as winners, for other kennels.

Meg Purnell-Carpenter's Overhill kennel is the only one of the three still active in the breed today. Very successful as a breeder and importer in the early days, producing foundation stock for many other kennels, including some of our own dogs, the Overhill kennel is

still producing typy Akitas today. Meg's dedication to the breed has meant her being respected as one of the top breed specialists and it culminated in her awarding CCs at Crufts 1998.

IMPORTANT SIRES AND DAMS
Imported from the USA by David (Killilea) in 1985, Am. Ch. The Real McCoy O'BJ became one of the most influential sires to date, appearing on many of the foundation pedigrees of today's leading kennels. Although McCoy hated the show ring and his

Ch. Lizda Zee Zee Flash, bred by David, was the first British-bred bitch to gain her title, winning her third CC on the same day the first British male Champion won his. She took BOB. *Photo: Hartley.*

Ch. Am. Ch. Goshens Heir Apparent At Redwitch: The second Akita to gain the title of Champion in Britain, and to date, the top-producing sire with seven Champion offspring. *Photo: Hartley.*

Ch. Redwitch Prince Consort At Stecal, owned by Carol Bevis and Steve Dutton.

Ch. Redwitch Secret Affair At Jocolda, owned by Joan and Dave Rushby.

Photo: Hartley.

Ch. Keskai First Class (left) and Ch. Keskai First Love winning BIS and Res. BIS at the Japanese Akita Association Championship show 1993. Bred by Sue and Kevin Sadler.

Photo: Hartley.

Ch. Redwitch Designer Label and Ch. Glenettrick Crown Jewel taking BIS and Res. BIS at the Akita Club of Scotland.

Ch. Claran Cailedh: Winner of 11 CCs. Bred and owned by Clare Andrews.

Pedigree of Ch. Goshens Bigger Is Better At Redwitch

Am Ch Karma–Ki's The Royal Sting

CH Goshens Bigger Is Better At Redwitch
Male
Red and Black White Markings
Born: May 9, 1992
Bred by: Pamela Peterson and Lewis and
Julie Hoehn

Am Ch Goshens Fire Dancer

Ch. Goshens Bigger Is Better in the Group
ring at Crufts 1994. Not only a top show dog
winning a total of 17 CCs, but a prolific sire
winning Top Sire 1994, 1995 and 1996, and
Top Stud 1997.

career as a sire was cut short, being sterile by the age of six, he played a dominant part in the strongest line of sires ever produced.

His own sire, Am. Ch. Okii Yubi's Sachmo of Makoto is still the Number One sire all-time in America, and McCoy's son, Am. Ch. The Widow Maker O'BJ is the Number Two sire all-time. Not surprisingly, from his first home-bred litter, came the first British-bred Champion bitch, Ch. Lizda Zee

		Am Ch. Yamakumos Itazura Sama
	Am Ch. Tobe's Abrakadabra	
		Am Ch. Tobe's Princess Leia Organa Cd
Am Ch. Karma–Ki's Ringside Rumor		
		Am Ch. Tobe's Adam Of Genesis
	Am Ch. Tobe's Snowstorm Barakuda	
		Am Ch. Sno Storm's Peking Jumbo Jet
		Am Ch. Tobe's Adam Of Genesis
	Am Ch. Tobe's Return Of The Jedai	
		Am Ch. Jag's Lois-T
Am Ch. Apogee's Cosmic Bombshell		
		Am Ch. Sherisan Ura Gin
	Am Ch. Goshens Jungle Jenny Of Noji	
		Am Ch. Kinouk's Kiss-n-Run
		Am Ch. The Widow Maker O'BJ
	Am Ch. O'BJ King's Ransom	
		Am Ch. The Mad Hatter O'BJ
Am Ch. Goshens Chariots O' Fire		
		Am Ch. The Real McCoy O'BJ
	Am Ch. The Dame's On Target O'BJ	
		Am Ch. The Same Dame O'BJ
		Am Ch. O'BJ King's Ransom
	Eng + Am Ch. Goshens Heir Apparent At Redwitch	
		Am Ch. Hikari's High Rope
Goshens Hot Wheels O'BJ		
		Am Ch. The Widow-Maker O'BJ
	Am Ch. O'BJ Canduit Tuya	
		Am Ch. The Mad Hatter O'BJ

Zee Flash, who remains the top producing dam to date.

Imported by the Killileas in late 1989 and without doubt the most prolific sire seen in this country to date was McCoy's great-grandson, Eng. Am. Ch. Goshens Heir Apparent at Redwitch. He joined us as America's No. 1 Akita and flew to his British title; but it was to be as a sire that Prince will always be remembered.

In his first year as a stud dog, Prince

Ch. Oktumi Valentine At Redwitch; From the double Champion breeding of Ch. Goshens Bigger Is Better At Redwitch to Ch. Keskai First Love. Litter sister to Ch. Oktumi Love Action. When sold to Dr Wayne Welsh in Barbados, she went on to become Top Dog All Breeds. 1997.

Photo: Dave Freeman.

Ch. Auberge Sir Duke At Stecal (Ch. Redwitch Prince Consort At Stecal – Brandeezi Prima Donna): The first of two Champions bred by Tony Fleetwood, campaigned to his title by Carol Bevis and Steve Dutton.

produced more top-winning puppies than any other dog and it was not long before some of these were winning CCs. Carol Bevis and Steve Dutton's Ch. Redwitch Prince Consort at Stecal took his first CC from the puppy class, went on to win Groups and Reserve Best in Show at Championship level and became a top producer in his own right, winning the Top Sire award in 1997. Prince Consort was to become one of seven UK champions produced by Prince. Sue and Kevin Sadler used Prince on their Anshee Storm Warning to Keskai, a McCoy grand-daughter, and produced two Champions in their first litter, Ch. Keskai First Class and Ch. Keskai First Love.

Mated to our own Ch. Goshen's Classy Sassy at Redwitch, Prince produced Ch. Redwitch Secret Affair at Jocolda, and to our Goshen's Dream on with Farmbrook we got Ch. Redwitch Designer Label.

Clare Andrew mated her Redwitch First Lady of Ikusmas to Prince to produce still one of the biggest winning bitches in Ch. Claran Caleidh, and the Scott family produced their first-ever

Ch. Auberge Brandywitch At Keskai: Litter sister to 'Duke', owned by Sue and Kevin Sadler.

Champion, Ch. Glenettrick Crown Jewel, when they mated Prince to Brandeezi Smart Remark.

It is without doubt that Prince left a legacy of top winners and top producers for all those who love this breed. He was Top Sire in 1991, 92 and 93 and Top Stud Dog in 92, 93, 94, 95 and 96, a record that will stand for many years to come.

Ch. Redwitch Kiss 'N' Tell from the quarantine-born litter by Am. Ch. Daijobu's Sting Of B Line to Goshens Wheels Of Fire. Her litter brother, Redwitch Kiss Me Quick, also became a Champion.

Ch. Redwitch Pure Velvet At Tanglemuir (The Steel Glove O'BJ Of Cheney – Ch. Lizda Zee Zee Flash): The first Redwitch-bred Champion, at eight weeks.

Ch. Redwitch Pure Velvet At Tanglemuir winning her crowning CC at Manchester 1993 under judge Joan Rushby.

Following in his great-grandfather's footsteps came Prince's stablemate, Ch. Goshens Bigger Is Better At Redwitch. Digger was fortunate in that he had the Prince daughters and grand-daughters to breed to. As a show dog he was exceptional, but he soon began to make his mark as a sire. Producing the top winning bitch to date, Ch. Oktumi Love Action and our own Ch. Oktumi Valentine at Redwitch out of one of Prince's Champion offspring, Ch. Keskai First Love, he also has several other CC-winning progeny. He was Top Sire in 1994, 1995 and 1996 and Top Stud Dog in 1997.

Quite a few dams have produced double Champion litters. Meg Purnell-Carpenter's Overhills Kita Mouri was exported to America, bred to Am. Ch. The Widow Maker O'BJ and brought back through quarantine in whelp. She produced Meg's Ch. Overhills Cherokee Lite Fut and Angela Rickard's Ch. Overhills Wituwa at Freestead.

Tony Fleetwood bred Brandeezi Prima Donna at Auberge to Ch. Redwitch Prince Consort at Stecal to produce Ch. Auberge Sir Duke at Stecal and Ch. Auberge Brandywitch at Keskai.

From a quarantine-born litter, we bred Ch. Redwitch Kiss-Me-Quick and Ch. Redwitch Kiss 'N' Tell out of Goshens Wheels of Fire, and as previously mentioned, Sue and Kevin Sadler's Ch. Anshee Storm Warning to Keskai produced litter brother and

The Japanese Akita Association Championship show 1997: Pictured (left) BIS Ch. Nor. Ch. Redwitch Dancin' In The Dark (Akita breed recordholder with 28 CCs) and Res. BIS Ch. Oktumi Love Action (Akita bitch recordholder with 21 CCs).
Photo: Alan V. Walker.

sister, Ch. Keskai First Class and Ch. Keskai First Love, who then went on in turn to produce two more Champions, Ch. Oktumi Love Action and Ch. Oktumi Valentine at Redwitch, bred by Carl and Shirley Jones.

However, the top producing dam of all-time to date is the McCoy daughter, Ch. Lizda Zee Zee Flash. Her first litter to The Steel Glove O'BJ produced Ch. Redwitch Pure Velvet at Tanglemuir. In her second litter, when bred to Heir Apparent, she produced Ch. Redwitch Prince Consort at Stecal and with another change of sire, this time Ch. Goshen's Dark 'n' Debonaire at Redwitch, came Ch. Nor. Ch. Redwitch Dancin' in the Dark and litter sister Ch. Redwitch Dancing Queen at Mandait. Although we are justly proud of Zee's progeny as top winners, above all she gave us temperaments. She was, without doubt, one of the sweetest Akita bitches we have owned and this legacy lives on through her offspring.

BREED DEVELOPMENT

It has take over fifteen years for a recognised type to come to the fore in the Akita in this country. Because, in the early days, importers brought in lines from different kennels and from all over the USA, there was a very wide divergence in type in the original dogs.

Early breedings proved that certain lines did not 'click', with exaggerations in faults such as large pointed ears and snipy muzzles. Bad fronts and weak rears were the norm rather than the exception. More recently, the breed has progressed tremendously in these departments, with more thought being given to breeding programmes. The use of line-bred dominant sires was of tremendous benefit, with each one benefiting from the one before, as the quality of the offspring improved with each generation.

THE CARE PROGRAMME

Hereditary problems were also seen for

the first time in some of the early breedings, with entropion and hip dysplasia occurring far too often. Although this breed was special to those of us who owned them, we were now realising that the Akita was no different to many other breeds, in that it did have some health problems and greater care needed to be taken with selective breedings.

With the formation of the breed clubs came also a care programme, with encouragement towards the British Veterinary Association hip-scoring and eye-testing schemes and a recording of some of the health problems. This proved a great success, with most caring breeders taking part. However, for the scheme to succeed, all newcomers to the breed should be encouraged to continue with these programmes for the sake of the Akita's health.

At this time there were also several recorded cases of severe skin problems, but many of these could be attributed to lack of knowledge about housing and feeding the Akita. Many coat and skin problems can be caused by allergies, not only through the feed, but also by bedding and the home environment, e.g. nylon carpets, "shake 'n' vac" air-fresheners and detergents, to name but a few.

Now, with careful selection of a puppy from a responsible breeder, there is no reason why the Akita should not be as healthy as any other breed. Whether buying a top-quality show prospect or the perfect family pet, only the finer points should differ – the health, fitness and temperament of the day should be the same.

REGISTRATIONS
From 1981, when the first of the modern-day Akitas was registered in the UK, the breed showed an upward trend each year, reaching a peak in 1989 with 713 Akitas registered. From then on, registrations dropped slightly and then levelled off until 1995 when there was a remarkable upsurge, with numbers almost double that of any of the previous five years. We can only speculate as to the reason for this sudden increase, but a possible explanation could be that Akitas were, by then, regularly being awarded Group placements at major Championship shows throughout the country, including Crufts, so pushing the breed more and more into the limelight. In 1997, there were 1319 Akitas registered with the Kennel Club.

Indeed, this upward trend was reflected in the show ring. From the original seven entered in the Any Variety classes at Crufts 1984, 1998 had a record entry of 173 Akitas for Meg Purnell-Carpenter to judge. Also noticeable was the interest by the general public, with hardly a gap in the crowd at the ringside and people standing four or five deep, straining for the best view. The British show scene is one of the most competitive in the

A micro-chip scanner showing the dog's registration number clearly imprinted.
Photo: Keith Allison.

world and the Akita is now accepted by top judges as a real competitor for top honours. From Groups to Best in Show, from puppy stakes to Champion stakes, the breed is consistently to the fore and a real force to be reckoned with.

HELP AND EDUCATION

The Akita is now well represented by three breed clubs, all officially recognised by the Kennel Club. The Japanese Akita Association covers the whole of the UK, the Japanese Akita Club of Scotland represents the interests of those 'north of the border', while the Japanese Akita Club of Wales plays its part for our Welsh neighbours.

These clubs organise and run educational events, not only for present Akita owners, but for those considering purchasing an Akita in the future. These events are invaluable for the potential or novice owner, as there are still very few knowledgeable people in the breed in this country and professional help with information and training is still very hard to find. However, for the serious enthusiast, who takes the time and trouble to learn, there is a far better chance of succeeding in the breed than there ever was when David and I first sought help and advice.

OVERFLOWING RESCUE

On the downside, the Akita has recently been the target of much bad publicity. We are very firmly of the opinion that there are no bad dogs, only bad owners. Unfortunately, this does not help when the Akita is falling into the wrong hands and being used to promote the macho man image.

They are also being exploited by those with no love for the breed, only for what monetary gain they can make. This is not a new phenomenon; many other attractive new breeds have suffered in their hands, and we are left to pick up the pieces. The official Akita Rescue sanctuaries are often full to overflowing, a sad but true fact with a breed still very much in its infancy.

A relatively new innovation is that of micro-chipping or tattooing. We strongly support these schemes, believing that if a dog falls into the wrong hands and finishes in a rescue sanctuary or pound, the dog can be traced back to its original breeder, who should then take responsibility for it. If you do not have the facilities or finances to take back those that you have brought into the world, *you should not breed in the first place.*

FULL CIRCLE
It is testimony to the way the breed has improved in the UK that most imports of the last few years have not made the same impact as earlier ones. It is also interesting that exports to all parts of the world have risen, with British-bred Akitas winning top honours in many foreign parts, indeed even in America.

As interest in the breed grows, so the thirst for knowledge follows. More and more enthusiasts are taking the time and trouble to make the trip to the USA to see the Akitas and talk to top breeders. More books are available on the breed and, in this modern world, the internet is playing its part in helping owners with their research.

Currently, the Akita is on an up swing as far as the dedication and enthusiasm of the breeders is concerned. It has been shown that these dogs can live quite happily in the home environment and so the pet market has increased. However, we must not become complacent. As we grow older and new enthusiasts take our place, care must be taken that they have the same love and dedication to promote the breed or it will go into a decline. Although we can do without the popularity explosion that German Shepherd Dogs, Rottweilers and Afghan Hounds experienced, for the breed to retain its type, soundness and that special something that says Akita, the registrations must remain stable and the commitment of its guardians remain intact.

14 *THE AKITA IN AUSTRALASIA*

In 1986 Noel Lamb and Gary Prendiville registered the New Zealand Kennel Club's first Japanese Akita. He was NZ Ch. Kiskas Tatsumaki, imported from the UK. Later the same year, Noel and Jacqui Lamb imported another dog, NZ Ch. Kiskas Chenko, from the UK.

The following year, 1987, Diane Murray brought over a dog, NZ Ch. Lizda Atlantic Flyer, also from the UK, and in 1988 a bitch, NZ Ch. Burgoynes Tatami (UK), who was in whelp to an American dog recently imported into the UK, Am. Ch. The Real McCoy O'BJ.

It is interesting to note that several influential dogs imported to New Zealand from the UK are directly descended from American bloodlines.

The majority of early New Zealand imports were sourced from the UK. Akitas from the Kiskas kennel formed the foundation for Noel and Jacqui Lamb's Akitzu Kennel in Auckland, and

also Gary Prendiville's Toronga Kennel in Auckland. Puppies from Diane Murray's bitch, brought into New Zealand in whelp, went on to be foundations for her own Sakura Kennel in Invercargill, and also Jill and Logan Linton's Linden-Grange Kennel in Auckland, V. Lawler-Karaka's kennel in Palmeston North and Margaret Hippolite's Kodo Kennel in Nelson.

Up to May 1997, there have been nineteen imports from Australia, fifteen from the UK and one from the USA, making a total of thirty-five imports and a total of three hundred and twenty-nine Japanese Akitas registered with the New Zealand Kennel Club.

There have also been two litters from frozen semen, one dog whelped on April 13th 1993 from Kiskas Kodiak of the UK and two bitches whelped on October 1st 1995 by Am. Ch. Regalias Darq Wolf of the USA.

In 1998, Regalias One Sided Affair was imported in whelp, via Australia,

Am. Ch. Darq Horse Lauclair: Imported from Canada by Margaret Hippolite.

giving birth to eight puppies in quarantine, and a Canadian dog, Am. Ch. Darq Horse Lauclair, arrived, both imported by Kodo kennels.

SHOW SUCCESS
New Zealand has had four Akitas awarded Best in Show at All Breeds Championship level. The first was NZ Ch. Kiskas Tatsumaki. The most successful to date is the bitch, NZ Ch. Redwitch High Hopes from the UK. 'Kiri' has received three Best in Show awards and also was placed two years running at the most prestigious show in New Zealand, the NZKC National, taking Best in Group in 1994 and then Intermediate in Show in 1995. NZ Ch. Shaze Blade Warlord has one Best in Show and NZ Ch. Kodo Lone Star is probably the youngest, taking his award from the Junior class at twelve months.

New Zealand's first Akita Obedience title was gained by NZ Ch. Akitzu Pal Power CDX in 1992.

With quarantine regulations becoming less stringent and the advance in frozen semen techniques, New Zealand and Australian breeders should soon have more options when choosing bloodlines. Used wisely, this could mean more exciting times for the Akita breed in New Zealand.

NZ Ch. Redwitch Secret Weapon (Ch. Am. Ch. Goshens Hair Apparent At Redwitch – Ch. Goshens Classy Sassy At Redwitch).

A lovely head study of NZ Ch. Redwitch High Hopes. Owned by Margaret Hippolite.

AUSTRALIAN AKITAS

The first Akitas arrived into Australian quarantine on June 17th 1982. They were from the O'BJ Kennel in USA and were imported by Ken and Thelma Taylor of Kyooma Kennels, South Australia, a bitch, O'BJ Ink Spot and a dog, O'BJ Rocky. These Akitas had been exported via the UK, having to spend six months in quarantine there, and then a further three months in Australian quarantine.

O'BJ Rocky achieved several firsts for the breed. He was the first to be awarded a Challenge Certificate and at that very same show was the first Akita to be awarded Best in Show. Rocky was aged two-and-a-half years at the time. He was the first to gain his Australian title, on March 25th 1984, but unfortunately, he did not ever produce a litter and died aged eleven-and-a-half years. O'BJ Inkspot underwent surgery in the UK for a broken leg suffered in transit from America and was placed in a pet home in Australia.

Replacements were ordered from the USA and in October 1982 the bitch O'BJ Scarlet arrived, and then in November 1983, a dog, O'BJ Aces High. From these two dogs came the first Akita litter born in Australia, a litter of eight puppies whelped on June 7th 1984. Many more Akitas followed with imports from both the USA and the UK.

Pat and George Hall's Hallysium Kennel whelped a litter in March 1986 from Aus. Ch. Ellysium Princess Shikishi of the USA, sired by O'BJ Aces High. This litter went on to set many records for the breed and provide foundations for some of Australia's best-known kennels. Pat Hall's dog, Aus. Ch. Hallysium Sockit Tumi CDX, was the first Akita to receive dual Obedience and Championship titles, and her bitch from the same litter, Aus. Ch. Hallysium Classy Akiri CD, was awarded Best Bitch and Opposite Exhibit in Show at the prestigious Sydney Royal in 1988.

These two Akitas were later sold to Phil Thompson in Western Australia where Tumi features strongly in many pedigrees of the well-known Aarak Kennels. From the same litter came Aus. Ch. Hallysium Smokey Joe, owned by Alan Molan of Lanzeon Akitas in New South Wales. Smokey Joe was awarded Best Exhibit at the New South Wales Inaugural Akita Open Show in 1992 and, along with his son, Aus. Ch. Lanzeon Bronco Bill, has been

Aust. Ch. Jack Daniels At Redwitch (Ch. Goshens Bigger Is Better At Redwitch – Redwitch Hells Angel), owned by Lyn Keevers.

Aust. Ch. Hikays Brittany (Ch. Goshens Bigger Is Better At Redwitch - Redwitch Free Choice At Hikays).

extremely successful in the show ring. Aus. Ch. Hallysium Huggy Bear went to Jim and Renne Roche's Bendalock Kennel in New South Wales and Aus. Ch. Hallysium Bo Jangles went to the Robstan Kennels in Queensland.

The first Akita show in Australia was held on May 20th 1989 in Melbourne by the Akita Inu Club of Victoria Inc. and was judged by Mr L. Reeves of Victoria. Best Exhibit went to Akitako Ninja, bred by John and Hilda Francis of South Australia and owned by J Gales.

In more recent times, imports have dominated the show scene. Aus. Ch. Overhill's Swift of Fut, imported from the UK and owned by Jim and Renne Roche, was the first Akita to win Best in Show at a Royal Show in Australia and is undoubtedly Australia's top winning Akita to date, with his son, Aus. Ch. Bendalock Kiyojiro Go, following in his pawprints. Jeanette Meharry and Louise Dorr's Loujen Kennel in Queensland qualified two Akitas for the Dog of the Year contest in 1998 by taking Best in Shows at qualifying shows. Lyn Keever's bitch, Aus. Ch. Hikay's Brittany and Aus. Ch. Jack Daniels at Redwitch, both imported from the UK, are consistent winners around the New South Wales shows. NZ Aus. Ch. Kodo Kreme de Koko from New Zealand has set a record, taking Bitch Challenge at the Melbourne Royal and Victorian Akita Specialty for three successive years.

In both Australia and New Zealand, the Akita breed is regularly awarded top honours in the show ring. This can be attributed to the dedication of the breeders who have shaped the breed in the past and who have had the foresight to import bloodlines and undertake breeding programmes for the future.